THE ILLUSTRATED EVOLUTION OF THE GRAND PRIX & F1 CAR

SIMON READ

VELOCE PUBLISHING PLC
PUBLISHERS OF FINE AUTOMOTIVE BOOKS

Other Veloce publications -

Colour Family Album Series
Bubblecars & Microcars by Andrea & David Sparrow
Bubblecars & Microcars, More by Andrea & David Sparrow
Citroen 2CV by Andrea & David Sparrow
Citroen DS by Andrea & David Sparrow
Lambretta by Andrea & David Sparrow
Mini & Mini Cooper by Andrea & David Sparrow
Vespa by Andrea & David Sparrow
VW Beetle by Andrea & David Sparrow
VW Bus, Camper, Van & Pick-up by Andrea & David Sparrow

SpeedPro Series
How to Blueprint & Build a 4-Cylinder Engine Short Block for High Performance by Des Hammill
How to Build a V8 Engine Short Block for High Performance by Des Hammill
How to Build & Power Tune Weber DCOE & Dellorto DHLA Carburetors by Des Hammill
How to Build & Power Tune Harley-Davidson Evolution Engines by Des Hammill
How to Build & Power Tune Distributor-type Ignition Systems by Des Hammill
How to Build, Modify & Power Tune Cylinder Heads by Peter Burgess
How to give your MGB V8 Power by Roger Williams
How to Power Tune the MGB 4-Cylinder Engine by Peter Burgess
How to Power Tune the MG Midget & Austin-Healey Sprite by Daniel Stapleton
How to Power Tune Alfa Romeo Twin Cam Engines by Jim Kartalamakis
How to Power Tune Ford SOHC 'Pinto' & Sierra Cosworth DOHC Engines by Des Hammill

General
Alfa Romeo Owner's Bible by Pat Braden
Alfa Romeo Modello 8C 2300 by Angela Cherrett
Alfa Romeo Giulia Coupe GT & GTA by John Tipler
British Cars, The Complete Catalogue of, 1895-1975 by Culshaw & Horrobin
Bugatti 46/50 - The Big Bugattis by Barrie Price
Bugatti 57 - The Last French Bugatti by Barrie Price
Chrysler 300 - America's Most Powerful Car by Robert Ackerson
Cobra - The Real Thing! by Trevor Legate
Daimler SP250 'Dart' by Brian Long
Fiat & Abarth 124 Spider & Coupe by John Tipler
Fiat & Abarth 500 & 600 by Malcolm Bobbitt
Ford F100/F150 Pick-up by Robert Ackerson
Grand Prix & F1 Car, Evolution of the by Simon Read
Lola - The Illustrated History (1957-1977) by John Starkey
Lola T70 - The Racing History & Individual Chassis Record New Edition by John Starkey
Making MGs by John Price Williams
Mazda MX5/Miata Enthusiast's Workshop Manual by Rod Grainger & Pete Shoemark
MGA by John Price Williams
Mini Cooper - The Real Thing! by John Tipler
Nuvolari: When Nuvolari Raced ... by Valerio Moretti
Porsche 356 by Brian Long
Porsche 911R, RS & RSR by John Starkey
Porsche 914 & 914-6 by Brian Long
Rolls-Royce Silver Shadow/Bentley T Series, Corniche & Camargue by Malcolm Bobbitt
Rolls-Royce Silver Wraith, Dawn & Cloud/Bentley MkVI, R & S Series by Martyn Nutland
Schumi, Michael Schumacher by Ferdi Kraling
Singer Story: Cars, Commercial Vehicles, Bicycles & Motorcycles by Kevin Atkinson
Triumph TR6 by William Kimberley
Triumph Motorcycles & the Meriden Factory by Hughie Hancox
Volkswagen Karmann Ghia by Malcolm Bobbitt
VW Beetle - Rise from the Ashes of War by Simon Parkinson
VW Bus, Camper, Van, Pickup by Malcolm Bobbitt

First published in 1997 by Veloce Publishing Plc., 33, Trinity Street, Dorchester DT1 1TT, England. Fax: 01305 268864.

ISBN: 1 874105 91 X/UPC: 36847 00091 2

Readers with ideas for automotive books, or books on other transport or related hobby subjects, are invited to write to Veloce Publishing at the above address.

British Library Cataloguing in Publication Data -
A catalogue record for this book is available from the British Library.

Typesetting (Optane), design and page make-up all by Veloce on AppleMac.
Printed and bound in the UK.

Contents

Introduction

Pared of non-essentials, and designed to specific technical requirements, today's Formula One cars represent the pinnacle of international motorsport and the leading edge of automotive design.

In just one century, these machines have evolved into cars of great complexity, through a process of continuous innovation driven by fierce competition and ever-increasing commercial pressure for success.

The result is an incredible array of unique designs that are artistically striking and technically fascinating.

Each machine is connected by a common thread across decades of motorsport, and this book follows the connecting thread from the earliest motor races and cars, through all the major events and milestone developments that have influenced the evolution of the F1 cars to today's form.

Simon Read

Chapter 1 Origins

1895 Panhard et Levassor
▼

In June 1895, the Automobile Club de France (ACF) organised what is generally regarded as the first internationally contested motor race. The race, from Paris to Bordeaux and back, covered a distance of 745 miles.

Of the twenty-two starters, only nine cars completed the course. After a drive of over forty-eight hours, the Panhard of Emile Levassor was the first

1902 Gordon Bennett Napier

1903 Mors 'Dauphin'

to return. However, Levassor's special two-seater failed to secure an official win, with victory going to the first four-seater to finish, some six hours behind. Controversy, it seems, has never been far from motor racing!

Levassor's Panhard used a four cylinder Daimler engine that provided 4hp to turn the chain driven rear wheels via a three-speed gearbox. A steering tiller directed the wooden chassied car.

In the years that followed, as the motor industry began to grow, it became clear that racing provided opportunities to develop cars and promote them before an increasingly interested public. In 1900 James Gordon Bennett, an American newspaper magnate living in Paris, financed a series of races conceived as a contest between national teams. The Gordon Bennett Trophy races, held on closed public roads, helped establish the popularity of circuit racing, and were the forerunners of modern Grand Prix competition.

National racing colours derived from this period. Green, originally the chosen livery of the victorious Napier team of 1902, was then adopted by subsequent British entries. The white of Mercedes, which became silver in the 1930s, was taken up by the other German teams. The Belgian national teams used a yellow colour scheme; blue became the French racing colour, American teams used lighter blue with white and the Italians embraced the famous racing red in which Ferraris are clad to this day.

The victory of Selwyn Francis Edge and his 6.5-litre shaft driven Napier brought the series to Ireland, as the winning British nation had the honour of hosting the annual event the following year.

The spectacular city-to-city races continued throughout Europe until the notorious Paris to Madrid run of 1903. The event was prematurely halted at Bordeaux, after several accidents injured spectators as well as competitors. Emille Mors won the shortened race with his pressed steel chassis, four cylinder Dauphin. The car was notable for its aerodynamic bodywork and finned tube radiator, demonstrating considerable evolution over such a short period of competition.

Chapter 2 The first Grands Prix

1906 Grand Prix Renault
▼

The Gordon Bennett Trophy races limited each nation to three entries per race. By 1905 France had achieved such supremacy as a motor manufacturer that this restriction was regarded as unreasonable. When Leon Thery's victory meant that France would host the 1906 race, the ACF

1907 Grand Prix Fiat

refused to organise the event. In its place they inaugurated a Grand Prix race, staged over two days around a 64 mile course at Sarthe, near Le Mans, which became an annual meeting open to all comers.

The first Grand Prix winner was the Hungarian driver, Franz Zsiz, at the wheel of a powerful 13-litre shaft driven Renault. In the June heat on rough dirt roads the cumbersome machine completed over seven-hundred miles at speeds approaching 70mph.

A year later the Association Internationale des Automobile Clubs Reconnus (AIACR), based in Paris, oversaw the organisation of further national Grand Prix events.

Development of the cars centred on the engines, specifically increasing power and efficiency. Wheels with detachable rims were popular as they facilitated quick tyre changes. The riding mechanic became as important as the driver, monitoring instruments and operating fuel and oil pumps.

Fiat enjoyed great success with their 16.3-litre chain driven behemoth. In the hands of Felice Nazzaro the Italian team dealt heavy blows to French pride.

1908 saw widespread use of dropped frames to lower overall height. New bodywork designs with built up and scuttles, at last, offered some protection to the crews. The first service pits were provided (literally, trenches at track level).

Chapter 3 David and Goliath

The onset of a world trade recession brought an end to Grand Prix racing by 1909. Smaller, more economical cars were then developed, principally in France. Usually framed around a 3.0-litre engine capacity, they became known as voiturettes.

Voiturette racing rose to prominence with events such as the Coupe de L'Auto, a series that limited the maximum cylinder bore to 80mm. It soon became apparent that the light cars performed excellently, and that reduced weight offered advantages over sheer power. The power to weight ratio was, for the first time, considered of vital importance.

1910 Lion Peugeot Voiturette

In order to increase engine power without exceeding the cylinder bore restriction, the Lion Peugeot featured a huge piston stroke. The result was an enormously tall engine set in a low slung frame.

Bugatti led the field in the design of lively and efficient voiturettes. The Type 13 and its derivative, the Type 22 Brescia, seriously challenged all opposition. In addition, they were quite capable of running with the heavyweight cars when Grand Prix racing resumed in 1912.

For these GP events the only major

▲ **1911 Bugatti Type 13**

stipulation was a width restriction of 175cm. The period witnessed titanic battles between the large-engined heavyweights and the lighter voiturettes. The massive 14-litre four cylinder Fiat was very competitive, although regarded as somewhat traditional by 1912 standards. It was an imposing machine, the most brutish of the early Grand Prix cars.

Widely considered to be the first modern Grand Prix car, the 1912 Peugeot featured a high-revving 16 valve, four cylinder engine of 7.6-litres. The advanced layout, which used twin overhead camshafts, worked well and clearly defined the direction of future development.

By 1914 most teams had adopted similar engines. Regulations for that year limited total capacity to 4.5-litres. Mercedes added hemispherical combustion chambers to their twin overhead cam four cylinder engine, and produced a more powerful and reliable unit. In addition, the rear axle design created an inward camber of the rear wheels that enhanced traction on corners.

At the outbreak of the First World War, racing halted in Europe, but continued in the USA.

1911 Fiat S74 ▼

1912 Grand Prix Peugeot

1914 Grand Prix Mercedes

Chapter 4 Straight eight and monoposto

Grand Prix racing began again in Europe after the war, at first based around the 3.0-litre regulations popular in the USA. However, by 1922, the AIACR restricted engine capacity to 2.0-litres with a minimum overall weight set at 650kg.

With the aim of extracting increased power from smaller engines, the supercharger was devised. A belt driven pump mounted beside the engine forced air under pressure into the cylinders. The increased volume of air enabled the combustion of a richer fuel mixture, offering greater power - but with the price of higher fuel consumption.

1923 Fiat 805/405 Corsa

▲ **1926 Bugatti Type 35**

Fiat introduced the system to mainstream racing in 1923. The straight eight cylinder 2.0-litre engine used a single supercharger to produce 130bhp.

A year later a number of European Grands Prix, run under the regulations set down by the AIACR, formed a low-key World Championship series. By 1925, riding mechanics were banned and driving mirrors became obligatory.

For 1926 the AIACR limited overall weight to 700kg. In an attempt to curb engine power they also restricted capacity to 1.5-litres, but this had little effect as development continued, with superchargers often mounted in pairs.

Offset driving seats began to appear, with propshafts passing through the position previously occupied by the riding mechanic. This layout enabled the chassis - along with the centre of gravity - to be lowered.

In the age of the 1.5-litre straight eight, Bugatti was most successful. Defying convention, the car used cast alloy wheels with integral brake drums. From 1928 to 1930, the larger 2.3 and 2.65-litre Bugatti Type 35Bs, in the hands of Louis Chiron and, later, Achille Varzi, dominated Grand Prix racing.

Another manufacturer from the voiturette age rose to supremacy in 1927: for that season Delage eclipsed even the mighty Bugatti. The car featured the now familiar layout of eight cylinders with twin overhead camshafts and twin superchargers.The only other car to come near Bugatti or Delage was the Mercedes, with its advanced straight eight supercharged twin cam. Designed by Dr Ferdinand Porsche, the Mercedes

1927 Delage Straight Eight ▶

engine utilised four valves per cylinder, sodium cooled exhaust valves and dry sump lubrication. However, the chassis handled poorly in comparison and a number of fatal accidents sullied the car's reputation. Mercedes merged with Benz in 1926.

In 1928 engine restrictions were abandoned due to falling entries. The principle rule stipulated a weight of

1927 Grand Prix Mercedes ▼

▲
1932 Alfa Romeo Tipo B P3

between 550kg and 750kg. A year later the first Grand Prix was run through the streets of Monaco. Although originally greeted with scepticism, the event has become astonishingly durable and continues to be a memorable spectacle.

By 1930 all restrictions were abandoned. Formula Libre, as it was known, provided designers with greater freedom and led to mixed fields of stripped sports and pure racing cars. The doors opened for the inevitable production of the definitive single-seat racer.

The Alfa Romeo Tipo B, also known as the P3, was the first genuine single-seat racing car. The monoposto, built around a 2.65-litre twin supercharged straight eight, was famously campaigned by Tazio Nuvolari - widely regarded as the greatest driver of the period - for Scuderia Ferrari.

By 1933 the AIACR announced re-introduction of the 750kg weight limit for the 1934 Grand Prix events. The French and Italian teams decided that existing cars would serve with a few minor modifications. However, two German manufacturers conceived a fresh approach that would earn them total dominance in the years to come, their drivers - Rudolf Caracciola, Hermann Lang, Manfred von Brauchitsch, Luigi Fagioli, Hans Stuck, Herman Muller and Bernd Rosemeyer - becoming household names.

Chapter 5 The Silver Arrows

Further regulations applied to the 1934 events defined minimum cockpit dimensions and imposed a race distance of at least 312 miles (500km). The formula was designed to provide stability for the manufacturers over a period of three years.

The German government offered assistance to Auto Union and Mercedes-Benz in order that they could demonstrate their technical superiority through motor racing. They succeeded, mainly through new approaches to running gear and chassis design. Both

1934 Auto Union Type A

teams gained advantages in roadholding and handling, whilst continuing to develop already powerful engines. The silver cars swept all before them.

The legendary Auto Union Type A was the first mid-engined Grand Prix car, with a 4.4-litre supercharged V16 set between the driver and rear axle. The centrally positioned fuel tank ensured that handling remained consistent, as fuel level reduced.

The Mercedes-Benz supercharged straight eight twin cam was more orthodox, but with an extremely

▲ **1934 Mercedes-Benz W25**

1937 Mercedes-Benz W125 ▼

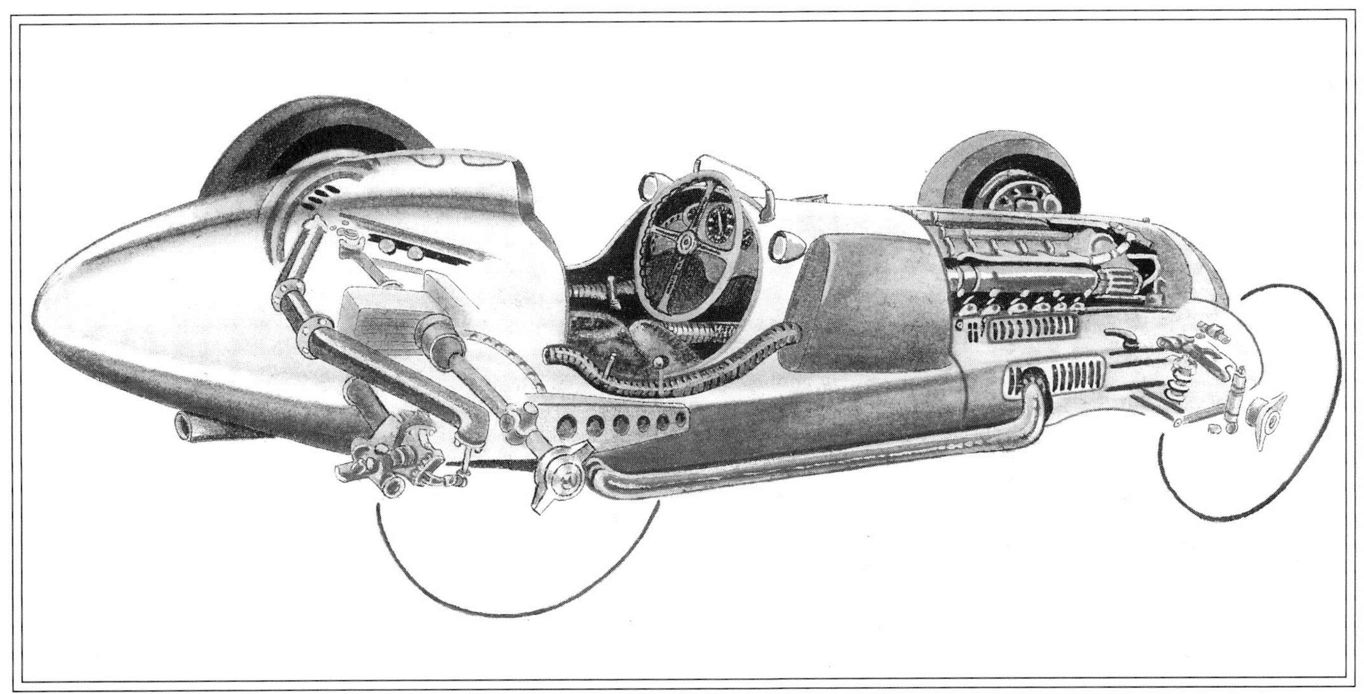

1938 Mercedes-Benz W154/163

innovative chassis. It combined all-round independent suspension with hydraulic brakes and a gearbox integral with the final drive.

In 1934 Auto Union began the season confidently and appeared to have the measure of all other cars, including Mercedes. The Type A achieved victory at the German, Swiss and Czech Grands Prix but, a year later, the W25s were dominant as Auto Union hit teething troubles with the Type B: Mercedes won eight of the 1935 events.

For 1936 Bernd Rosemeyer won four Grands Prix to become European Champion for Auto Union. The 750kg formula was extended to apply to 1937. Mercedes then introduced the W125, which featured a stiffer oval tube frame and revised suspension. The supercharged engine, by now capable of delivering over 600bhp, would remain the most powerful Grand Prix power unit ever seen until the turbocharged era of the 1980s.

For the 1938 and 1939 seasons, new legislation revised engine capacity in favour of normally aspirated engines of up to 4.5-litres, compared to the 3.0-litres allowed for supercharged blocks. This revision was too late for the French manufacturers, who collapsed before the German state-backed teams. Bugatti turned to sports car racing and, apart from a brief resurgence in the shape of Delahaye, French teams faded from the Grand Prix scene.

Both German teams developed two-stage supercharging, in which a small compressor fed a larger compressor before applying the total boost to the engine. Even with reduced capacity, the 3.0-litre V12 of the Mercedes-Benz W154 still produced around 480bhp, more than enough to ensure success.

1939 Auto Union Type D

Auto Union also built a new 3.0-litre, two-stage supercharged V12, but suffered the loss of Bernd Rosemeyer, who was killed in January 1938 during a speed record attempt for Auto Union.

By the following year the fourth version of the mid-engine design featured a de Dion rear axle like the Mercedes-Benz, and a revised camshaft layout. The Type D secured victory at the last pre-war Grand Prix, held in Belgrade shortly before the outbreak of the Second World War. When racing resumed in Europe in 1946, German industry was shattered: Auto Union were finished forever and Mercedes-Benz in no state to compete.

Chapter 6

The Italian renaissance

Since 1935, when driving genius Tazio Nuvolari, in a P3, beat the Germans on home soil, it had become clear that nothing could compete on an equal basis with Auto Union or Mercedes. The strongest challenge came from the Maserati 8C. The 3.0-litre, supercharged straight eight, mounted in a box-section chassis, was simple by comparison but ran strongly against the German machinery. The 8C later became the

1938 Maserati 8C

1938 Alfa Romeo 158/159 Alfetta

basis of the Boyle Specials that greatly influenced racing in the USA after victories at Indianapolis in 1939 and 1940.

Most teams concentrated on lesser formulae, where the lessons learned from lighter, smaller engined machinery would be put to good effect after the war. 1.5-litre supercharged units like the Alfa Romeo 158 enjoyed much success. During the war Alfa Romeo continued to test and develop the little Alfa, or Alfetta, as it was known. An improved chassis and two-stage supercharging increased the performance of the straight eight twin cam. When the Wehrmacht took control of northern Italy in 1943, seven Alfettas were hidden in a cheese factory in the remote mountain village of Melzo.

The Alfetta emerged to become the leading car of the post-war revival. From 1947 to 1951, it remained a front runner, chiefly by squeezing more and more power from the engine. The first two-stage supercharged units developed 225bhp in 1947 and up to 425bhp by 1951. The cost of this power increase was high fuel consumption, which finally fell to 1.6mpg.

In 1946 the ruling body had become the Commission Sportive Internationale (CSI) of the Federation Internationale de L'Automobile (FIA). Four years later the FIA formally introduced the Formula One Grand Prix Championship for Drivers. Points were awarded for the first six places as follows: 9-6-4-3-2-1. Race distances varied from two hundred to a little over three hundred miles, with the exception of the Indy 500 mile event which was included in the Formula One calendar until 1960.

Ferrari and Alfa Romeo were immediately the dominant teams and Giuseppe Farina, piloting an Alfetta,

1952 Ferrari 500

became the first World Champion after a season-long battle with team mate Juan Manuel Fangio.

In 1951 Ferrari began to develop normally aspirated engines with excellent torque characteristics. For the seven race series, Ferrari mounted the only challenge to the all-conquering Alfettas. However, with three wins, Fangio secured his first title and the last championship for Alfa Romeo.

1953 Maserati A6 GCM

In 1952 new Formula One regulations were announced by the FIA, intended for implementation for the 1954 season to allow the teams some development time. In the interim, 2.0-litre normally aspirated cars were allowed to compete.

The simple four cylinder 2.0-litre Ferrari 500 was already a well proven design in lesser formulae. Ferrari were better prepared than most when the World Championship races were thrown open to this class of car: in the hands of Alberto Ascari, the Ferrari 500 swept the board. With six victories in 1952 and five in 1953, Ascari became the first double World Champion.

Juan Manuel Fangio campaigned strongly for Maserati in 1953 after losing much of the previous year recovering from a broken neck, following an accident at Monza. The

▲ **1954 Mercedes-Benz W196 Streamliner**

2.0-litre, six cylinder Maserati A6 often threatened the Ferrari, winning the Italian Grand Prix for Maserati that year.

In 1954, post-war Formula One allowed engines of 2.5-litres normally aspirated, or 750cc supercharged, a ruling that effectively killed off the supercharger.

Mercedes-Benz returned to Grand Prix racing with the W196, a machine that, with its enclosed wheels, resembled a sports car and featured many expensive innovations, such as desmodronic valve gear. The engine, effectively the last straight eight, was set at an angle of 37 degrees in the spaceframe chassis. Difficulties with placing the wheels on tight corners resulted in the all-enveloping bodywork being replaced with a more conventional open wheeled design, except for at high speed circuits like Avus and Monza. (The FIA later formally banned full-width bodywork).

Mercedes-Benz began their 1954 campaign at the French Grand Prix at Rheims, the third of an eight race series. Juan Manuel Fangio had already won in Argentina and Belgium for Maserati, and joined Mercedes to win a further four races and his second World Championship.

Tragically, the first fatality of the Formula One World Championship occurred at the Nurburgring in August 1954 when Juan Manuel Fangio's replacement at Maserati, respected compatriot, Onefre Marimon, was killed during practice for the German Grand Prix.

The slipper-bodied W196 of 1955 repeated the success of the previous year. Maserati and Lancia were competitive and challenged hard, but the partnership of Juan Manuel Fangio and Stirling Moss remained unbeatable in all but one event of the six race

1955 Mercedes-Benz W196 Slipper Body

series. With four wins to his credit, the Argentine ace won his third World Championship.

In June 1955 Pierre Levegh's Mercedes-Benz 300SL, a 3.0-litre sports car derivative of the W196, hurtled off the Le Mans pit straight and somersaulted into the crowd, killing

1956 Lancia Ferrari D50

eighty-nine people. As a result of the worst accident in motorsport history, Mercedes-Benz withdrew from racing at the end of the year.

In 1956, following the death of Alberto Ascari in a testing accident, financially troubled Lancia handed over its racing department to Ferrari. The Lancias then wore the prancing horse emblem as Ferrari extensively developed the cars.

Juan Manuel Fangio joined Lancia-Ferrari for 1956 to drive the V8 2.5-litre D50, the car featuring double choke carburettors and twin fuel tanks fitted in sponsons rigged each side. He achieved three victories, and team mate, Peter Collins, a further two, making this a superb season for Lancia-Ferrari and the Argentine driver, who won his fourth title. The D50 began to decline in competitiveness the following year, with Ferrari phasing it out by the close of the season.

Maserati introduced a straight six twin cam in a multi-tubular spaceframe for the 2.5-litre formula of 1954. The car won its debut race and proved immensely popular with private teams. In addition to fielding a works team, Maserati built thirty-two 250Fs for privateers; virtually mass-production for a Formula One car. Although generally outclassed by Mercedes-Benz, the Maserati was usually runner-up and dominated many non-championship events of the period. With two wins in 1956, the 250F was the most serious challenger to Lancia-Ferrari.

When Juan Manuel Fangio returned to Maserati in 1957, he added a further four victories on his way to a remarkable fifth World Championship. Thereafter, Maserati did not field a works team, although privately entered 250Fs ran in major events until 1960.

1957 Maserati 250F

Chapter 7

The mid-engine revolution

1958 Vanwall VW10

▼

For 1958 the FIA reduced race distances to 300km. Alcohol-based fuels, in popular use since the 1930s, were banned in favour of aviation gasoline. The FIA also introduced the Constructors' Cup, which represented a World Championship for manufacturers.

Juan Manuel Fangio scored his last Grand Prix points in a privateer 250F, taking fourth place at Rheims in July 1958. By this time Alfa Romeo, Lancia

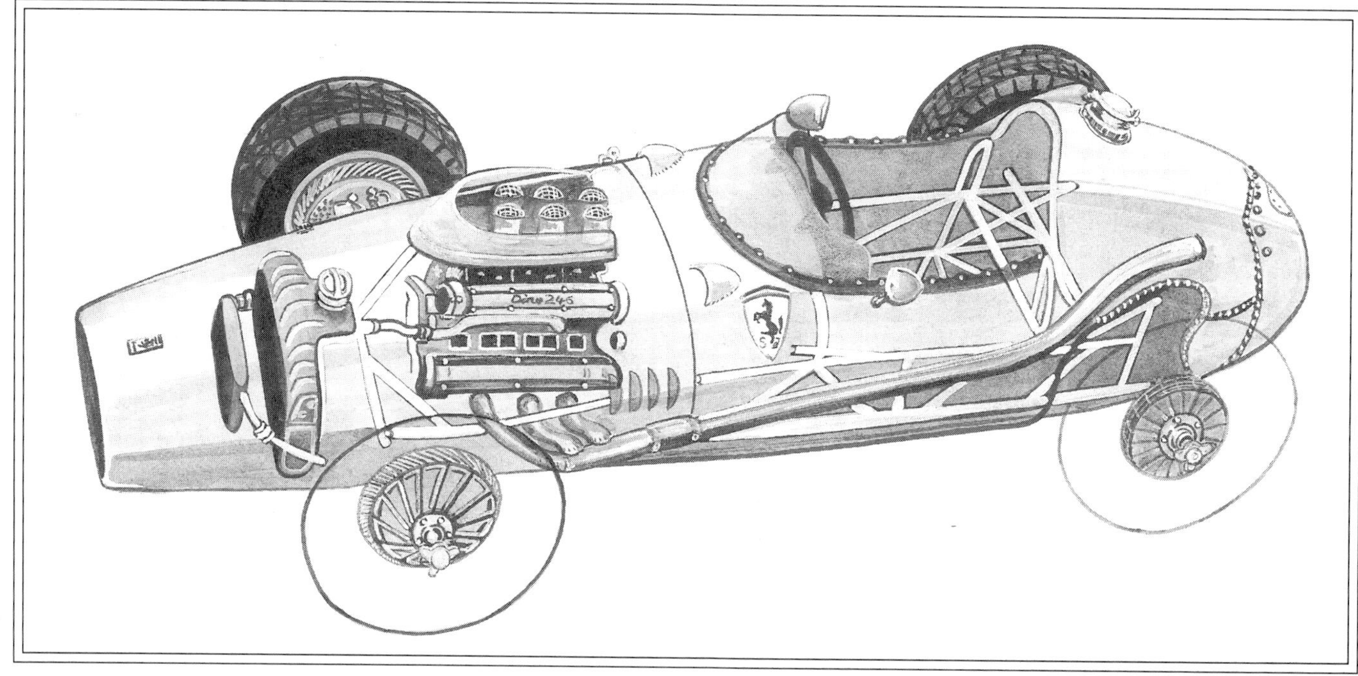

1958 Ferrari 246 Dino

and Maserati had withdrawn, leaving only Ferrari to uphold Italian racing honour. Porsche had entered Formula Two versions of their sports cars and were sole representatives for Germany.The other teams that scored points in 1958 - BRM, Cooper, Lotus and Vanwall - were all British: a new force had arrived ...

The Cooper Climax Formula Two derived T43 won the Argentine Grand Prix at the start of the season with Stirling Moss at the wheel. With this car Cooper had re-introduced the mid-engine layout, not seen since the days of the Auto Union.

Ferrari driver, Mike Hawthorn, became the first British World Champion, narrowly beating Stirling Moss by one point, despite having only one victory to Moss' four. Stirling, at least, had the consolation of helping Vanwall to the first Constructors' Cup with his three wins for them, matched by team mate Tony Brooks.

The Vanwall VW10 used a 2.5-litre, four cylinder engine with fuel injection, mounted in a spaceframe designed by Colin Chapman, and clad in smoothly styled, low drag bodywork. Six victories made it the class of the field in 1958.

Mike Hawthorn's Ferrari of 1958 was the last successful front-engine car; a single win and a string of second places gaining him the title that year. Ferrari mounted the 2.5-litre V6 at an angle in the tubular spaceframe chassis, in a way, similar to the earlier Mercedes Benz W196. The following year Ferrari could do nothing about Cooper and, by 1960, the Ferrari 246 was simply obsolete. However, Phil Hill scored his first win for Ferrari, and the last for the Dino, as late as the Italian Grand Prix of 1960.

In 1958, three drivers lost their lives

1959 Cooper T51

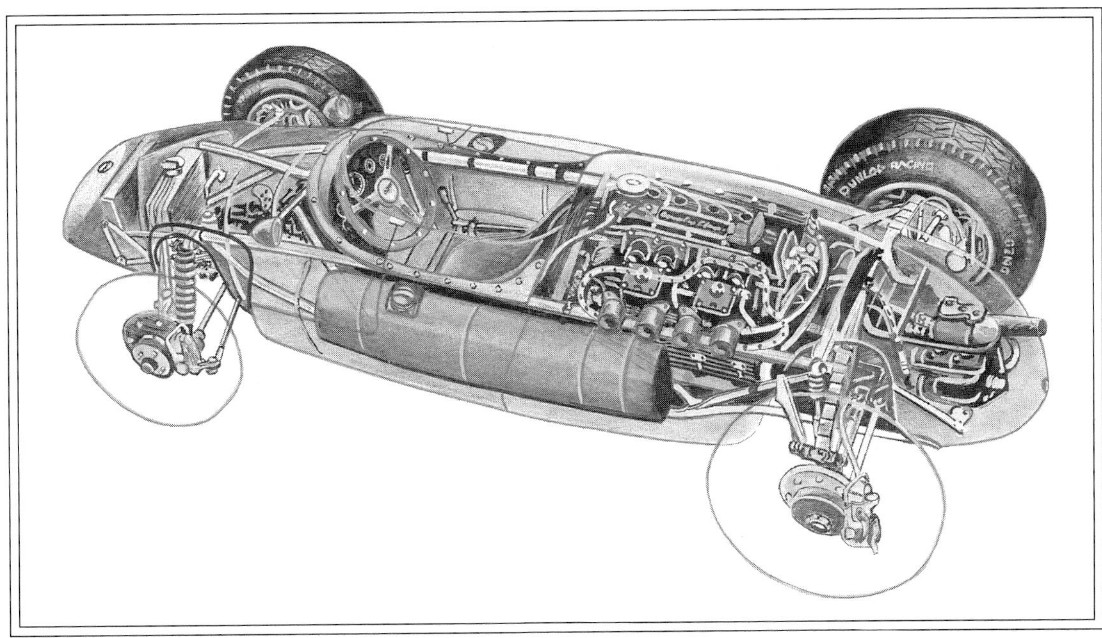

during Grands Prix: Luigi Musso in France, Peter Collins in Germany and Stewart Lewis-Evans at the Moroccan event.

For 1959, Cooper introduced the 2.5-litre T51. The full Formula One-sized development of the T43 took Jack Brabham and Stirling Moss to first and third place in the Drivers' Championship, and netted Cooper the Constructors' Cup. Other teams began to take the unusual little car very seriously indeed ...

1961 Ferrari 156 Sharknose

A year later, most F1 cars were using the mid-engine layout and Lotus, in particular, broke new ground with sophisticated suspension systems. However, Cooper maintained the competitive edge with Jack Brabham taking them to a second Constructors' Cup and his second Drivers' Championship.

British drivers, Chris Bristow and Alan Stacey, were killed during the 1960 Belgium Grand Prix.

For 1961, engine capacity was limited to 1.5-litres, which effectively upgraded the current F2 cars. The mid-engine Ferrari 156, dubbed the 'sharknose', carried a 1.5-litre V6 in a spaceframe chassis.

Ferrari interrupted British domination of the Constructors' Cup when their drivers achieved five wins from the eight race series. Phil Hill of the USA became World Champion after his popular team mate, Wolfgang Von

1962 Porsche Type 804

Trips, was killed, along with eleven spectators, during the Grand Prix at Monza.

Porsche competed for two seasons as a manufacturer in F1, their car having a 1.5-litre, flat-8 air-cooled engine with a large fan mounted above it. The beautiful, short wheelbase spaceframe design of the 804 was, sadly, rarely a front runner, although it was capable of great pace on occasion. After two victories and a string of points finishes, Porsche withdrew at the end of 1962 in order to concentrate on sports car racing. The 804 was the last F1 car to sport the silver livery of the German national racing teams until Mercedes returned in 1997 with McLaren.

The small, 1.5-litre F1 cars era produced some memorable racing, and saw the rise of many great drivers. Development revolved around chassis improvement and great strides were made in chassis construction, culminating with the introduction, by Lotus, of the monocoque design Type 25 (Gabriel Voisin pioneered - without success - monocoque construction of a racing chassis back in 1923). The tubular spaceframe remained the universally accepted method of construction until Colin Chapman decided to apply methods derived from the aviation industry. The monocoque was essentially a tub built from light alloy sheets, riveted together to form the central chassis section. The major components attached directly to the tub. This important advance offered huge advantages over the spaceframe in terms of rigidity, lower weight and increased strength; the spaceframe's

1962 Lotus 25 Monocoque

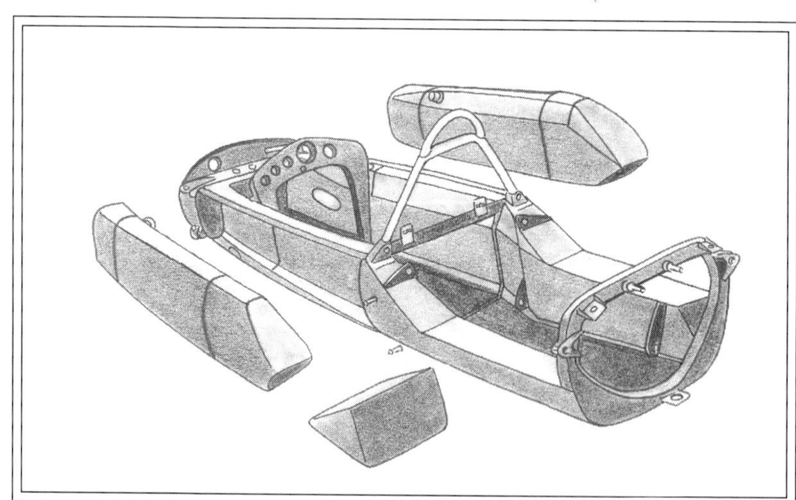

▲
1962 BRM P57 V8 Stackpipe

days were numbered ... Jim Clark won three Grands Prix for Lotus in 1962, but component failures gave the championship titles to Graham Hill and BRM in the final event of the nine race series in South Africa.

British Racing Motors mounted their 1.5-litre, 90 degree V8 in a lightweight spaceframe chassis with wishbone suspension and outboard brakes. Most entrants, at this time, bought in items such as engines and gearboxes, and only Ferrari and BRM manufactured all of the main components for their cars.

By 1963 Lotus had solved their reliability problems. Jim Clark was virtually unbeatable, taking seven wins from ten races, securing the World Championship and the Constructor's Cup for Lotus.

The following year an accident during practise for the German Grand Prix at the Nurburgring claimed the life of Dutch driver Carel Godin de Beaufort.

Lotus introduced the derivative Type 33 with larger wheels and improved brakes, in which Jim Clark challenged hard in 1964, losing out in the final event in Mexico to John Surtees and the Ferrari 158, which took the Constructors' Cup. A development of the 156, the 158, used an interim V8 engine before Ferrari adopted the well-

1963 Lotus 25
▼

proven V12 for the new 3.0-litre formula. The car, compact and tidy, was typical of the period and John Surtees and Lorenzo Bandini used it to good effect.

The Honda RA272 featured a 1.5-litre, V12 mounted - unusually - transversely to the monocoque in a tubular sub-frame. After a development year with the RA271, Honda achieved success in their second F1 season, when Richie Ginther drove the RA272 to victory at Mexico City.

The further improved Lotus 33 was far more convincing in 1965: Jim Clark took his second World Championship and Lotus gained another Constructors' Cup with six wins in the last year of the 1.5-litre formula.

1964 Honda RA272

1964 Ferrari 158

Chapter 8 The 3.0-litre Formula One

For the 3.0-litre formula of 1966, the FIA allowed only commercially available pump petrol. Onboard automatic starters became mandatory, along with roll bars, whilst streamlined bodywork which covered the wheels was officially banned. Oil replenishment during the race was no longer permitted and battery cut-out switches were introduced for the first time.

In 1966 Jack Brabham's third World Championship was achieved, uniquely, in a car bearing his own name. His triumph was soured when John Taylor, in his Brabham-BRM, fatally crashed at the Nurburgring. Brabham also took the Constructors' Cup in 1966 and 1967, with team mate Denny Hulme taking the Drivers Championship for 1967.

1966 Repco Brabham BT19

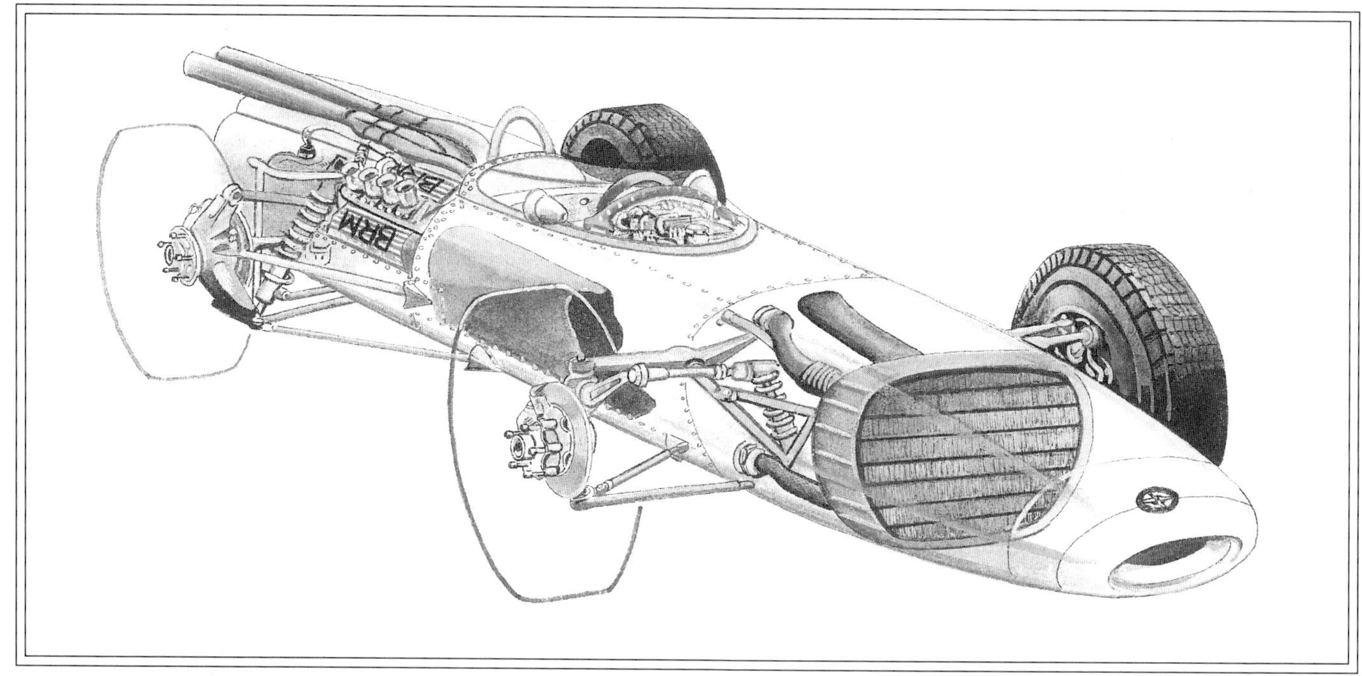

▲ **1967 BRM H16**

The BT19 used a spaceframe chassis, rather belatedly in view of the advancing monocoque trend. Based on an Oldsmobile unit, the Repco V8 offered a broad power range with useful torque. The engine had been conceived in 1964 and developed in time for the 3.0-litre formula. In 1966, Brabham were simply better prepared than other teams and preserved their momentum into 1967 with the improved BT24.

1967 saw emergence of some of the most beautiful cars ever to grace the Grand Prix racing circuits. V12s and V8s were most popular, set in longer and lower bodywork between fatter tyres. This generation of cars had an aggressive and purposeful demeanour.

Beneath the skin of the BRM H16, the sleek, full monocoque held an upright radiator behind the open nose. The complex suspension system, with inboard dampers at the front, carried large disc brakes. The exhaust pipes curved upwards and back across the top of the engine behind the tall roll bar, and fuel was stored each side of the cockpit in aviation-style bag tanks.

The 1967 Ferrari featured a light V12 block, installed in a monocoque chassis that extended far to the rear to support the engine. As the team developed it, the car became increasingly competitive until events at the Monaco Grand Prix shattered morale at Ferrari. Their charismatic star driver, Lorenzo Bandini, crashed out of second place during the closing stages, the car overturning and bursting into flames. Trapped in the wreckage, Lorenzo burned to death before anyone could help. Bandini's accident was attributed to fatigue, a conclusion that added to growing pressure for a full safety review.

Another striking design of the

▲ **1967 Ferrari 312-67 001**

period, the Eagle, was the product of Dan Gurney's Anglo-American Racers concern. The 3.0-litre, 60 degree Weslake V12 gave over 400bhp. The Eagle's light monocoque and conventional suspension bore much resemblance to the Lotus 38 Indycar which Gurney had helped to develop in 1965.

1967 Eagle Weslake T1G ▶

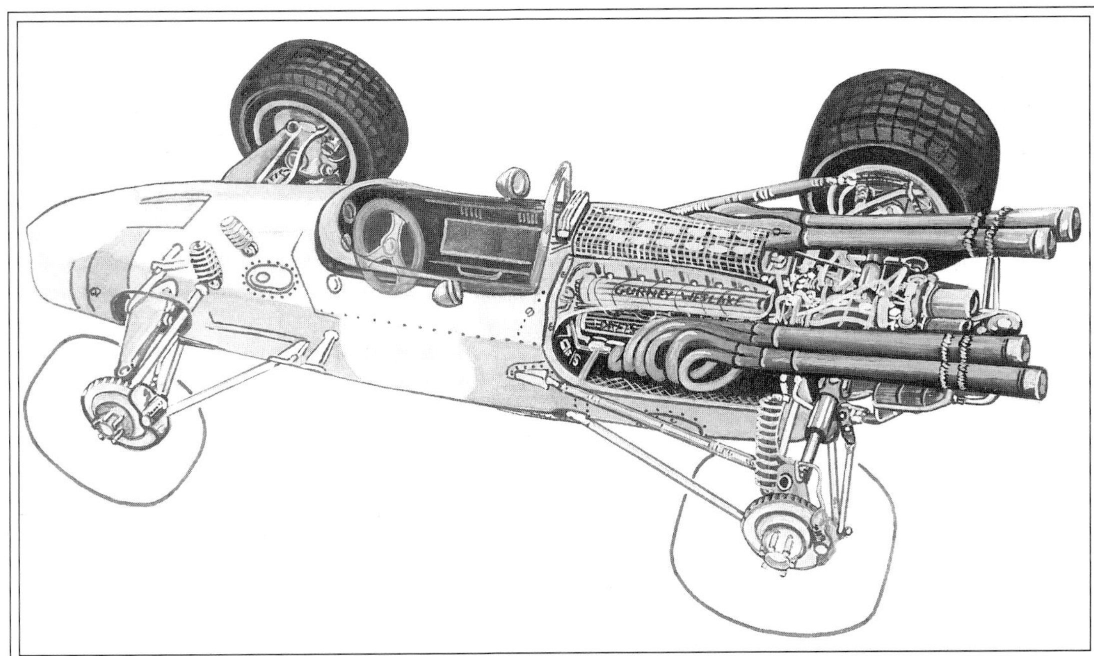

Chapter 9 Rise of the constructors

Colin Chapman conceived the plan to design and build a racing engine from scratch, securing funds from Ford and use of the unit for the Lotus team. Mike Costin and Keith Duckworth, of Cosworth Engineering in the UK, then developed the most durable power plant in motorsport. From introduction in 1967 to the 155th win at Detroit in 1983, the Ford Cosworth V8 became the key component of many front-running cars.

The construction decided upon for the engine was the 90 degree V8, known as the DFV (for Double Four Valve). The 3.0-litre block was neat and compact, producing 412bhp in 1967 and exceeding 480bhp by the 1980s. Introduced with the Lotus 49 in 1967, the Cosworth achieved a debut race win.

After a successful season with Lotus, Cosworth made the DFV available to other customers. This encouraged the growth of many new teams, enabling them to concentrate on chassis design around a ready-to-race competitive engine. From 1968, customer engines used Hewland transmission, although many of the new constructor teams carried out their own modifications to the gearbox, while others used them straight off the shelf. For more than a decade, small teams were able to compete successfully against huge corporate manufacturers.

The Lotus 49 was specifically designed around the Ford Cosworth DFV. By bolting the engine directly to the monocoque, Chapman was able to employ the V8 block and gearbox transaxle as a fully stressed, load-bearing extension of the chassis. With the suspension attached directly to the engine, there was no need for the additional weight of a rearward frame. By uncoupling the hoses and linkages, the entire rear half of the car could

▲ **1969 Lotus 49/B**

easily be removed. This important advance became central to all F1 car design by 1969.

Lotus failed to beat the Repco Brabham team in 1967, the new car not yet reliable enough to score consistently. A year later it set new standards, capturing the Constructors' Cup and taking Graham Hill to the World Championship. Tragically, Jim Clark had been killed earlier in the year while competing in a minor event at Hockenheim. The Honda driver, Jo Schlesser, also suffered a fatal accident in 1968, during the French Grand Prix at Rouen-les-Essarts, precipitating withdrawal from F1 of the Japanese company.

The Lotus 49 was the first car to be fully liveried in the colours of a

1968 Matra MS11 V12 ▼

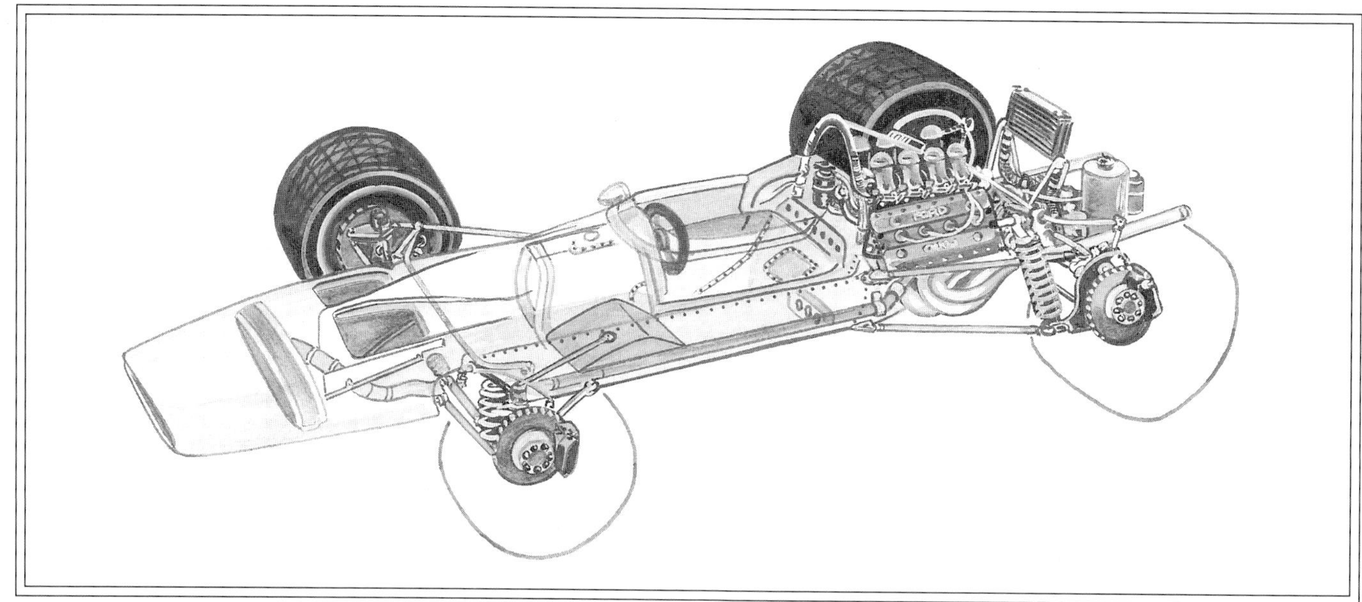

▲ **1968 McLaren M7**

commercial sponsor, the team being known as Players Gold Leaf Team Lotus. This arrangement, sneered at by some, is still recognisable today. At the centre of controversy in 1968, Lotus were the first to use the high strut-mounted wings; Ferrari and Brabham having experimented with more modest devices.

Ken Tyrrell entered Formula One in 1966 with a Matra chassis powered by a BRM unit. For 1967, Matra, the premier French aerospace company, and Elf Oil began work on a new, all-French F1 car. With French government backing, the Matra V12 was ready for 1968. The monocoque chassis was well constructed along conventional lines, except for the use of integral fuel tanks rather than the more commonly

1969 Matra MS80 ▼

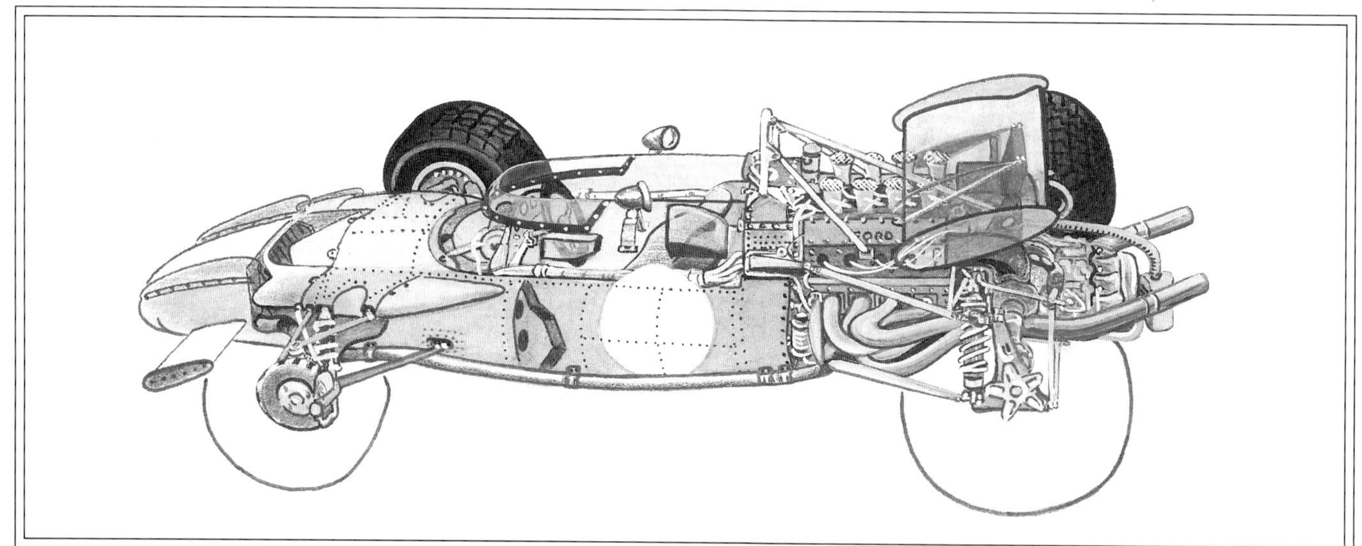

adopted flexible bag type. Noted for the ear-splitting exhaust howl of its powerful V12, the car suffered teething troubles and a consequent lack of concrete results, despite being a very impressive machine.

While running the MS11 V12, Tyrrell persuaded Matra to modify a chassis to accept the Cosworth DFV, enabling him to secure the services of the rising young star, Jackie Stewart. The Cosworth powered MS10 brought Matra success through Stewart's three victories and overshadowed the MS11. As a result, the V12 was thereafter applied to the Matra sports car programme while, for 1969, the Grand Prix team went over fully to the DFV.

At the age of twenty-two, New Zealander, Bruce McLaren, became the youngest ever Grand Prix winner when he drove a Cooper T51 to victory at the 1959 Sebring event. He founded Bruce McLaren Motor Racing Limited in 1963 and left Cooper two years later to build and race a very successful series of sports cars that dominated Can Am racing from 1967 to 1971.

McLaren's F1 cars yielded little initial success until the availability of the Cosworth gave the team the breakthrough it was seeking. The M7, designed by Robin Herd, utilised an open topped monocoque and conventional outboard coil spring and wishbone suspension. The M7 won the Race of Champions in 1968, its debut event.

Bruce McLaren and Denny Hulme took three victories between them and the team was runner-up to Lotus for the Constructors Cup. Sadly, Bruce was killed while testing a Can Am car at Goodwood in 1970. His long-time friend, Teddy Mayer, who had helped found the team, became the principal and went on to guide McLaren to greater glory in the years to come.

In 1969 Jackie Stewart won the first of his three World Championships with six wins and Matra took the Constructors Cup. The MS80 used integral fuel tanks each side of the monocoque and a fully stressed DFV that supported the rear suspension. The inboard rear brakes were cooled by scoops mounted above them and, by the closing stages of the season, new wings had been designed in accordance with the growing 'science' of downforce theory.

Matra then severed links with Ford and resumed development of their V12 for Grand Prix use. Tyrrell decided to build his own chassis for the 1970 season. While Matra steadily declined, Tyrrell and Jackie Stewart traded victories and championships with Lotus in an extraordinary battle encompassing six seasons of Grand Prix racing.

Chapter 10 Four wheel drive

The Cosworth DFV's popularity largely levelled the playing field with regard to power. Designers realised that chassis development deserved closer attention; improved traction translated power to performance more effectively. Many considered that four wheel drive would deliver the advantages sought, thereby making better use of the substantial torque of the DFV.

In 1968 Lotus narrowly failed to win the Indianapolis 500, after dominating the event with a pair of four wheel drive cars. Commissioned for the race by the STP Corporation, the dramatic, wedge-profile Lotus 56 looked unique among its contemporaries. Powered by a United Aircraft gas turbine engine, using axial compression, the 56 needed air brakes to compensate for the lack of engine braking.

For Grand Prix racing Lotus

1968 Lotus 56 Gas Turbine

▼

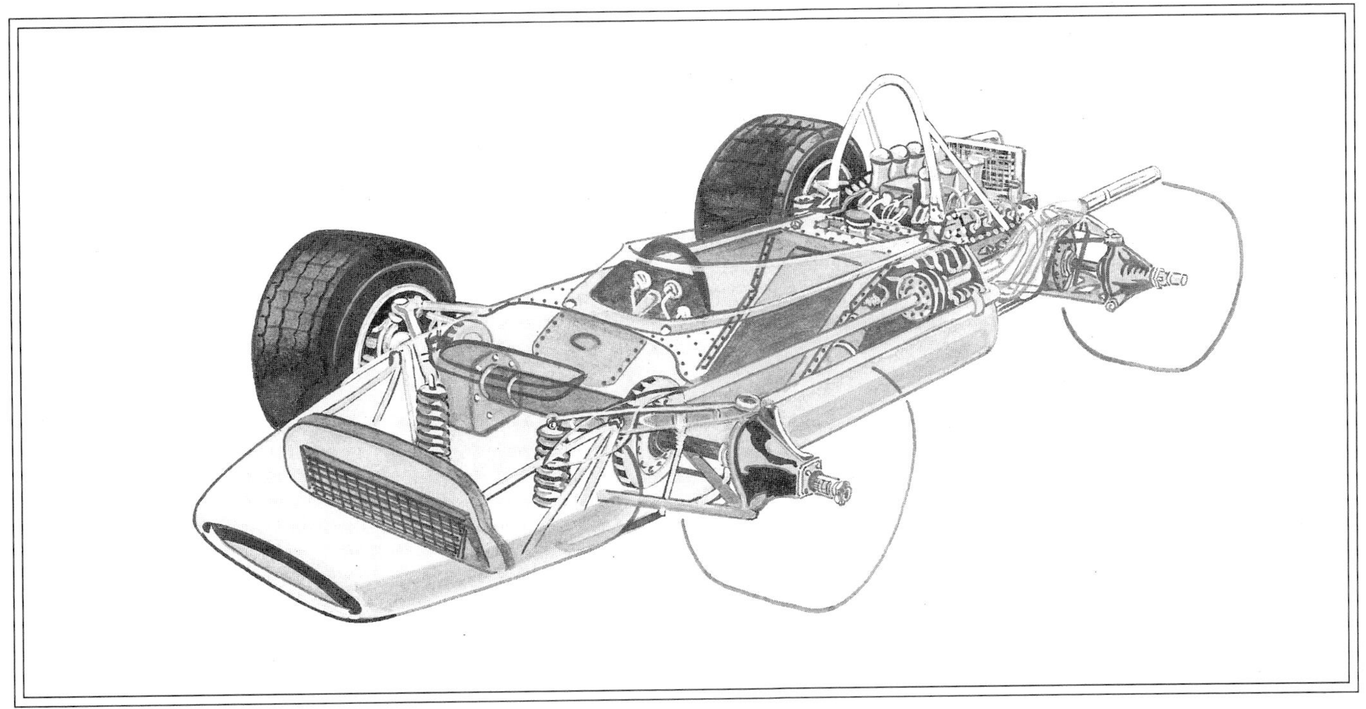

1969 McLaren M9A 4WD

developed a DFV powered version, the Lotus 63, but it was a complete failure and never raced. The 56 did take part in the Italian Grand Prix at Monza in 1971, but without success. Lotus then abandoned the programme in favour of a more conventional approach.

In addition to Lotus, Cosworth, Matra and McLaren also experimented with four wheel drive F1 cars and all met with costly failure. Transmission systems needed to be much more sophisticated to cope with the demands of four wheel drive. The extra driveshafts and linkages also meant extra weight. Advances in aerodynamics and improving tyre technology provided increased levels of traction for two wheel drive cars, resulting in the four wheel drive experiments being discontinued.

McLaren's M9A was typical of the four wheel drive experimental cars. The driveshafts linking front and rear wheel drive made the car too heavy to be viable. It raced only once, at Silverstone, in July 1969, before being withdrawn.

Four wheel drive was not actually banned until 1982, by which time materials technology had greatly advanced; kevlar and carbon fibre providing lightweight components of immense strength. In addition, very powerful turbocharged engines and computer telemetry were available. If four wheel drive had still been an option the story might have turned out very differently.

Chapter 11 Downforce

During practise for the Belgium Grand Prix of 1968, the Ferrari and Brabham teams fielded cars with wings. The devices were actually inverted aerofoils that generated negative lift, or downforce, when in motion. The teams mounted the wings high in the airstream over the rear of the cars, attaching them to points on the suspension. Under acceleration, the tyres pressed firmly to the track, greatly enhancing traction and therefore speed and cornering ability. Balancing vanes either side of the nose countered the lethal tendency of the winged cars to somersault over their own rear axle.

Quick to recognise the possibilities of this advance, Lotus led the aerodynamic devices race with more ambitious structures. The Type 49B adapted well to downforce devices and other teams soon followed suit. By the following year wings were attached to both front and rear suspensions on tall frames, referred to as the bi-wing arrangement. At the Spanish Grand Prix in May 1969, however, both 49Bs suffered rear wing collapses, leading to spectacular accidents, from which Graham Hill and Jochen Rindt were fortunate to escape without serious injury.

During practise for the next Grand Prix at Monaco, wings were abruptly banned by new regulations framed in time for the Dutch Grand Prix a month later. The height of the wing above the underside of the car was restricted to 80cm and overall width limited to 110cm.

Much lower and more secure rear wings soon began to appear over the engines of most cars and teams began to use larger front vanes. By 1970, wings had become a crucial element in all F1 car design.

Modern racing cars use the principles of flight to achieve their

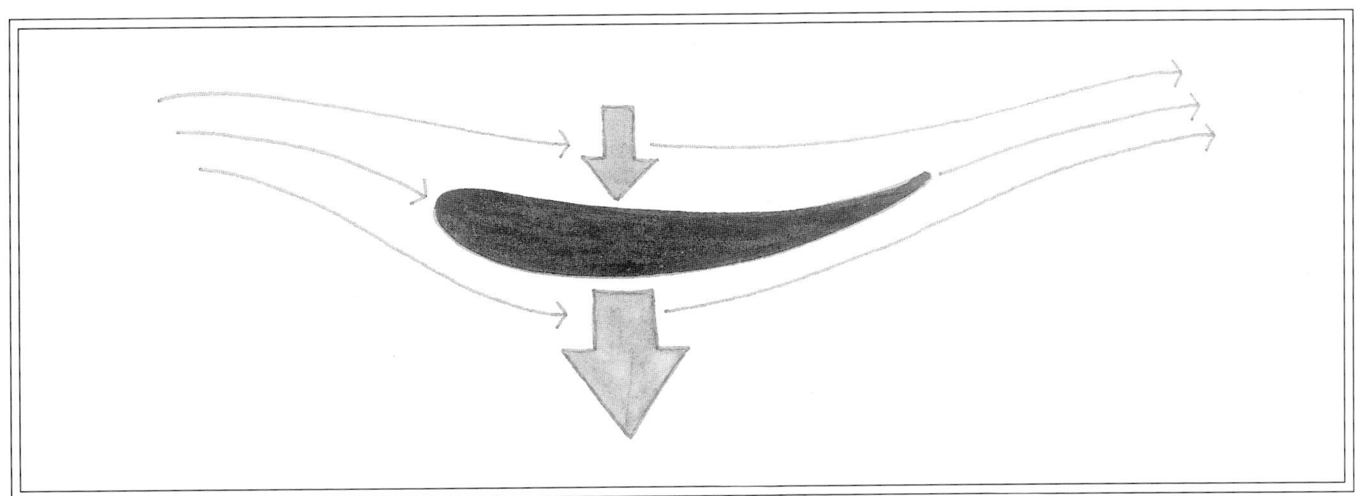

▲
Inverted wing cross-section

performance. Exactly as with an aircraft wing, the aerofoil shape generates lift as it moves through the airstream. As it is upside down, the force is a negative lift, or downforce. The curved underside of the racing wing causes air to flow across it at a faster rate than the air above, generating an area of lower pressure underneath the wing that draws it downwards.

With the wing cars of the eighties, this aerodynamic profile formed the basis of the chassis structure (see Chapter 15).

Chapter 12 The 3.0-litre evolves

By the late 1960s the wealth of structural innovation and increasing complexity of F1 cars, along with accidents experienced in recent years, led to concerns over safety. Designers found themselves beset by more legislation than ever. The sport was evolving from the pursuit of 'gentlemen racers' into an era of greater commercialism and technical expertise.

From March 1969, more substantial roll bars, onboard fire extinguishers and electrical circuit breakers became mandatory. Fuel filler caps were not to protrude above the coachwork, and the FIA also introduced a new minimumweight limit of 500kg to accommodate the extra safety equipment. By the end of the season, detailed restrictions were applied to aerodynamic devices. For 1970, rubber bag fuel tanks - already in widespread use - and monocoque construction, were also made mandatory.

Rapid advances in tyre technology began when Firestone challenged Dunlop's Grand Prix monopoly in 1964. A year later Goodyear joined the fray and fierce competition resulted in the development of softer compounds, around a wider and better constructed carcass.

The all-weather rubber tyres of the 1960s evolved into tyres for wet weather use, which retained tread patterns, and a new type suitable only for dry conditions. The 'slick' put the maximum area of rubber possible in contact with the track, greatly enhancing traction, but tending to aquaplane over a wet surface. Slicks came into widespread use during 1970 and 1971, by which time Dunlop had left Grand Prix racing. Three years later Firestone also gave up in the face of Goodyear's greater resources.

First raced at the opening event of 1970 at Kyalami, the handsome Ferrari

▲

1970 Ferrari 312B

1971 Lotus 72

▼

312B featured a three-quarter length monocoque bonded to an integral spaceframe. Out of the rear bulkhead a backbone projected, from which the engine was suspended. Developed and tested over the previous year, the horizontally opposed 12 cylinder 'Boxer' evolved into an extremely powerful unit, serving over a decade in Grand Prix racing. However, in 1970, Clay Reggazoni and Jacky Ickx could not prevent Jochen Rindt and Lotus from taking the championship titles.

In September 1970, Jochen Rindt lost his life in a Lotus 72 during practice for the Italian Grand Prix at Monza. With five wins to his credit, no other drivers were able to match his points total in the remaining races of the season, and Jochen was posthumously declared World Champion. Sadly, Piers Courage was also killed in 1970, during the Dutch Grand Prix whilst driving a Brabham entered by his close friend, Frank Williams.

Lotus introduced the long-serving Lotus 49's successor halfway through the 1970 season, and immediately set a new benchmark. In order to retain the aerodynamically effective wedge profile pioneered on the Type 56, Lotus dispensed with the usual nose mounted radiator in favour of smaller units on each side of the car. The hip radiators ensured reduced frontal area and removed a major heat source ahead of the cockpit. A cooler driver environment was further enhanced by siting the oil tank and coolers in the tail, giving greater rearward weight bias, adding load to the rear tyres. Inboard brakes reduced unsprung weight and kept heat away from the tyres, enabling softer compounds to be run for longer distances. Firestone co-operated with production of special rubber for the 72's tyres.

▲ 1971 Tyrrell 003

1972 Lotus 72/B JPS ▼

With the loss of Jochen Rindt, 1971 saw the Lotus team in poor spirits, development of the 72 making slow progress, and new drivers unable to achieve successful results.

Since introduction late in the 1970 season, the original Cosworth powered Tyrrell 001 progressed rapidly through a series of design modifications. The 001 featured a blade-like front wing above a shark mouth intake. To accommodate the tall Frenchman, Francois Cevert, a longer wheelbase version, 002, was built; halfway through 1971 003 arrived when the nose section was redesigned to a full-width bluff fairing.

In either guise Jackie Stewart used the Tyrrell to good effect, dominating the season by taking six victories, the 1971 World Championship and the Constructors' Cup for Tyrrell.

For 1972 regulations demanded 16 gauge sheet fuel tank protection, and also banned engines of more than twelve cylinders. Wet weather rear lights became mandatory.

With the new John Player Special livery over a revised rear wing and airbox, the Lotus 72 performed well during 1972. Emerson Fittipaldi battled all season with Stewart's Tyrrell, winning five events to Jackie's four to become the youngest ever World Champion at the age of twenty-five years and eight months. Lotus took their fifth Constructors' Cup; the second in three years with the Type 72. Another title for the team followed in 1973, this time on Goodyear tyres. The 72 was still winning races as late as 1974, although, by then, beginning to show its age.

The 1973 season saw the

1973 Tyrrell 006

1974 Brabham BT44

implementation of a 250-litre maximum fuel tank capacity, along with an increased minimum weight limit of 575kg. Deformable structures, able to absorb impact forces, were also introduced.

The Lotus versus Tyrrell duels continued as before. With five victories against seven between Fittipaldi and Peterson, Jackie Stewart claimed his third World Championship. After announcing his retirement at the end of the season, and scheduled to take part in his hundredth and last Grand Prix at Watkins Glen, Jackie Stewart withdrew when his team mate, Francois Cevert, was killed during practise. Earlier, the Dutch Grand Prix at Zandvoort had claimed the life of British driver Roger Williamson.

The last of the championship-winning Tyrrells featured a high trident airbox and hip mounted oil coolers. As had its main rival, Tyrrell sited cooling funnels over the inboard front brakes and out-rigged the large front wing as far as practicable. However, the 006, developed from the prototype 004 and less successful 005 of the previous year, retained a nose radiator within its wide front fairing.

Gordon Murray's 1973 Brabham BT42 offered a third alternative radiator siting, introducing split nose units, along with a novel pyramid section chassis. With aerodynamic improvements, the upgraded BT44 became a front runner in the second half of the 1974 season, with Carlos Reutemann driving the car to three Grand Prix victories.

Chapter 13 V8 versus Flat 12

For 1974 the FIA restricted rear wing overhang. Wings became more solidly mounted, most commonly on large, upright central posts. McLaren introduced a safety system that supplied the driver with oxygen in the event of being trapped in the car after an impact.

In the previous six years, the Lotus and Tyrrell teams had traded the championship titles back and forth; for the next four years, another British team was in the ascendancy and the most famous name in motor racing was also back on top.

As in all such cases, when cars with an effective design have risen to prominence, the fortunes of the teams owed much to the contribution of the drivers. When presented with a car that offered potential, they worked tirelessly to test and improve it. Besides the

1974 McLaren M23/B

ability to put in outstanding race performances, all winning drivers seem to possess the charisma to motivate a team to consistently high achievements. At various stages a handful of drivers dominated several seasons in different cars, and often different teams, much of the advantage explained only by their personal input. Driving style is also important; occasionally, a proven driver changes teams and totally fails to progress with a car that does not suit his technique.

Emerson Fittipaldi left Lotus for McLaren in 1974. The team had recently secured sponsorship from Texaco and Marlboro. The previous year had seen the unveiling of the M23, backed by Yardley Cosmetics, which Peter Revson drove to victory in Britain and Canada; team mate Denny Hulme also won in Sweden. In 1974 the modified chassis accepted rocker arm front suspension and parallel link rear suspension, with inboard coil springs and dampers. The brakes were outboard in front and inboard at the rear. Over the season the team also modified the Hewland transmission and experimented with different nose sections.

Fittipaldi collected three wins and Denny Hulme another, which gave McLaren the Constructors' Cup, just three points ahead of Ferrari. Fittipaldi won his first World Championship, again, by only three points, ahead of Ferrari's Clay Reggazoni. Austrian, Helmuth Koinigg, became the second fatality at Watkins Glen.

Clay Reggazoni and new recruit, Niki Lauda, had put up some strong performances with the 312B3. Upgraded beyond recognition from the 312 of 1970, the car now sported a full-width front wing, tall airbox and wider

1975 Ferrari 312T ▶

1976 McLaren M23/D ◀

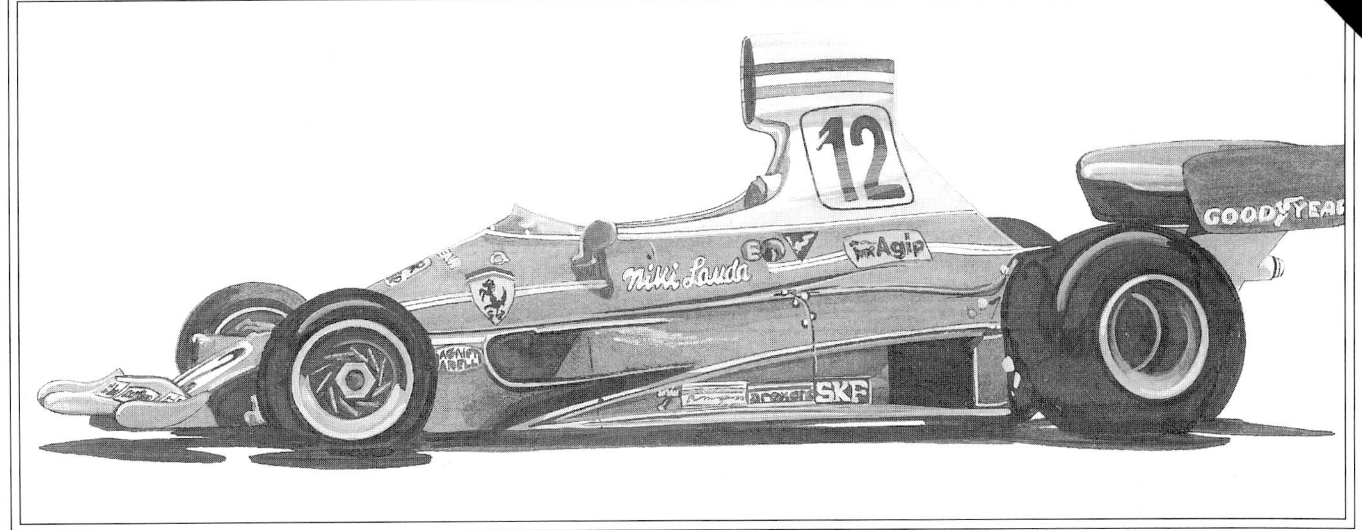

bodywork.

Seeking improvements for 1975, Ferrari decided to follow the example of Tyrrell and concentrate more mass within the wheelbase. This produced an extremely nimble car that felt nervous and required great skill to tame and use effectively, abilities that Niki Lauda. possessed in abundance.

The 312T, T for Trasversale, featured a transverse shaft gearbox mounted on the rear of the Flat 12 engine with most of the mass ahead of the rear axle line. Also within the wheelbase were oil coolers to the rear and radiators each side at the front: between them lay the large fuel tanks.

With the 312T, Ferrari became the first team to achieve a hat-trick of Constructor's Cups, taking the title from

1975 Ferrari 312T

...iki Lauda took his first ...nship with five wins in ...hat also saw the Cosworth-engined McLaren, Brabham, Tyrrell and Hesketh achieve victories. A further fatal accident marred the sport; American Mark Donohue was killed in Austria.

For 1976 further restrictions were applied to rear wing overhang, airbox height and tyres. Rear tyres were limited to a maximum width of 21 inches with a maximum wheel diameter of 13inches, whilst front wheel diameter was free of restriction. Overall width of the cars was not to exceed 215cm.

For its fourth re-make the McLaren Cosworth was upgraded and extensively modified to comply with new regulations. For the benefit of sponsors, the now-familiar Marlboro day-glo red livery was introduced, designed to enhance the car's TV identity as coverage was becoming more widespread.

The 1976 season was turbulent and controversial. In August Niki Lauda suffered horrific burns in an accident at the Nurburgring. Incredibly, he returned, six weeks after being given the last rites, to resume his title defence. McLaren and their number one driver, James Hunt, were penalised on numerous occasions due to alleged technical infringements. The season reached its climax in the final three rounds when James Hunt won in Canada and the USA. Finally, after a dramatic tyre change during a wet race at Mount Fuji in Japan, he snatched the World Championship from Niki Lauda by a single point. McLaren were unable to catch Ferrari for the manufacturers' title.

Up to this point all F1 tyres were of crossply construction. Casing plies of man-made textiles were laminated around the carcass and moulded into the rubber compound. In 1977, Michelin entered Formula One, initially with Renault, but also supplying Ferrari a year later. Having developed a range of radial ply road tyres, the French company introduced the product to Grand Prix racing.

In the belted radial, textile layers are built up across the tyre - at right angles to the direction of travel - supported by a steel or textile band moulded into the rubber capping beneath the working surface. Radials offered more traction, but deteriorated suddenly, compared to the gradual wear and loss of grip of the crossply. They also ran cooler and had better distortion characteristics, enabling softer compounds to be run, which meant more grip, and it soon became clear that this was the more effective tyre. After a brief withdrawal in 1981, Goodyear returned with their own radial ply tyres.

Niki Lauda's second World Championship followed in 1977, a season that saw a strong challenge from the new Walter Wolf team, originally founded by Frank Williams. Significantly, Lotus also returned to form, their innovative new design putting everyone else back to square one.

Chapter 14 Six wheels

1976 Tyrrell P34

▼

The Project 34 Tyrrell Cosworth of 1976 was very unusual, featuring four half-sized front wheels on specially made Goodyear tyres. The lower profile front section, with the little tyres barely intruding upon airstream, was designed to offer improved aerodynamic penetration.

Traction and braking capability were also enhanced by using an extra pair of front wheels.

To begin with it worked very well: the P34 finished in the points in most of the 1976 Grands Prix and pulled off a memorable one-two at Anderstorp in Sweden. However, in the following year, the rebodied P34s were excessively heavy and uncompetitive and Tyrrell decided to return to a more conventional chassis for 1978. The Tyrrell P34 was the only six-wheeled F1 car to actually race, although others were developed.

In 1977, March conceived and built a Grand Prix car with four smaller rear wheels, principally for aerodynamic reasons. All of the rear wheels were driven, designer Robin Herd adding a supplementary final-drive for the third axle in order to achieve four wheel drive traction. Despite encouraging test results, budget restraints prevented further development.

Late in 1981 Williams tested a similar layout with a converted FW07 chassis. Patrick Head later refined the driveshafts and side-pods to produce the FW08. It was found that traction and acceleration improvements, similar to those being sought through the earlier four wheel drive experiments, offered an answer to the challenge of the more powerful turbocharged teams. Williams suspected that the third axle could even accommodate slicks in wet weather, with wet tyres on the first two axles draining the track ahead. However, development progress during 1982 was slow; whilst the conventional four wheel version proved successful, the six-wheeler never started a Grand Prix. The governing body adjudged these cars to be four wheel drive machines and outlawed them under the legislation for 1983.

The six-wheeled cars were certainly interesting to look at. Perhaps the FIA was afraid that grids full of such exotic

1977 March 0-2-4

▲ **1981 Williams FW08 six-wheeler**

machinery might detract from the commercial appeal of Formula One. Whatever the reason for the ban, it seemed that nothing could prevent F1 cars from becoming steadily more complex. By the close of the 1977 season, another technical revolution was underway ...

Chapter 15 The ground effect wing cars

The Lotus 78, unintentionally designated a year ahead of its time, made its debut at the start of the 1977 season at Buenos Aires in Argentina. Mario Andretti won four Grands Prix that year and team mate, Gunnar Nilsson, added another, although engine failures and other mechanical faults kept Lotus behind Ferrari in the championship stakes. It was still a remarkable performance for a design in its development year so radically new. The result of extensive research into under-car airflow, the Lotus 78 was the first of a new generation, the wing car.

A bizarre and tragic accident during the South African Grand Prix again served to highlight the dangers of the sport. The Shadow of Tom Pryce collided with a marshal carrying a fire extinguisher across the track; the heavy cylinder struck the driver and killed him instantly.

1977 JPS Lotus 78

1978 JPS Lotus 79

Wing car design used full-length, wide side-pods, with an aerodynamic profile, providing a boxed section open to airflow front and rear but sealed to the track by flexible skirts. The inverted wing cross-section of the side-pods created low air pressure under the car, compared with high air pressure over the upper bodywork. In the same way that an aircraft wing generates lift in an airstream, the inverted wing-shaped pods generated negative lift, or downforce. The 'ground effect', as it came to be known, literally sucked the car to the track. Mario Andretti described the road-holding of the Lotus 78 as "painted to the road".

The Lotus 79 took the ground effect concept still further. Spring-loaded sliding skirts with ceramic trailing edges made a more effective seal. Lotus moved fuel storage from the side-pods to a cell between the cockpit and engine and kept the redesigned rear suspension out of the airflow. The front suspension members, also made as neat as possible, provided for clean airflow to the side-pods. The narrow, upright block of the Cosworth DFV formed the ideal size and shape for smooth incorporation into the design.

Swedish driver, Ronnie Peterson, replaced compatriot, Gunnar Nilsson, after his death from cancer.

Mario Andretti and Ronnie Peterson each won a Grand Prix in 1978 before introduction of the 79 a third of the way through the season. The 79 proved the outstanding car of the year, Mario taking a further five victories and Ronnie also winning again. The pair finished at the front in one-two formation on four occasions before Ronnie Peterson's fatal accident at Monza. Stand-in driver, Jean Pierre Jarier, underlined the qualities of the Lotus 79 when he took pole position at Montreal in only his second race with the car. Mario Andretti became World Champion and Lotus took the Constructors' Cup by a huge margin, ahead of nearest rival Ferrari.

Ferrari number one, Carlos Reutemann, had achieved four victories

1978 Ferrari 312T3

and new recruit, Gilles Villeneuve, secured his first win on home ground at Montreal. The 312T3 was a handsome evolution of the Flat 12 design that enjoyed a fine season. However, ground effect technology outpaced Ferrari and every other team: they would have to design totally new machines for 1979 in order to remain competitive.

The Brabham BT46, using the Alfa Romeo Flat 12 engine, also ran strongly in 1978 against all but the Lotus 79. Designer, Gordon Murray, spotted a loophole in the regulations and the team set to work on a highly modified BT46 that was ready in time for the Swedish Grand Prix. The BT46B Fan

1978 Brabham BT46/B Fan Car

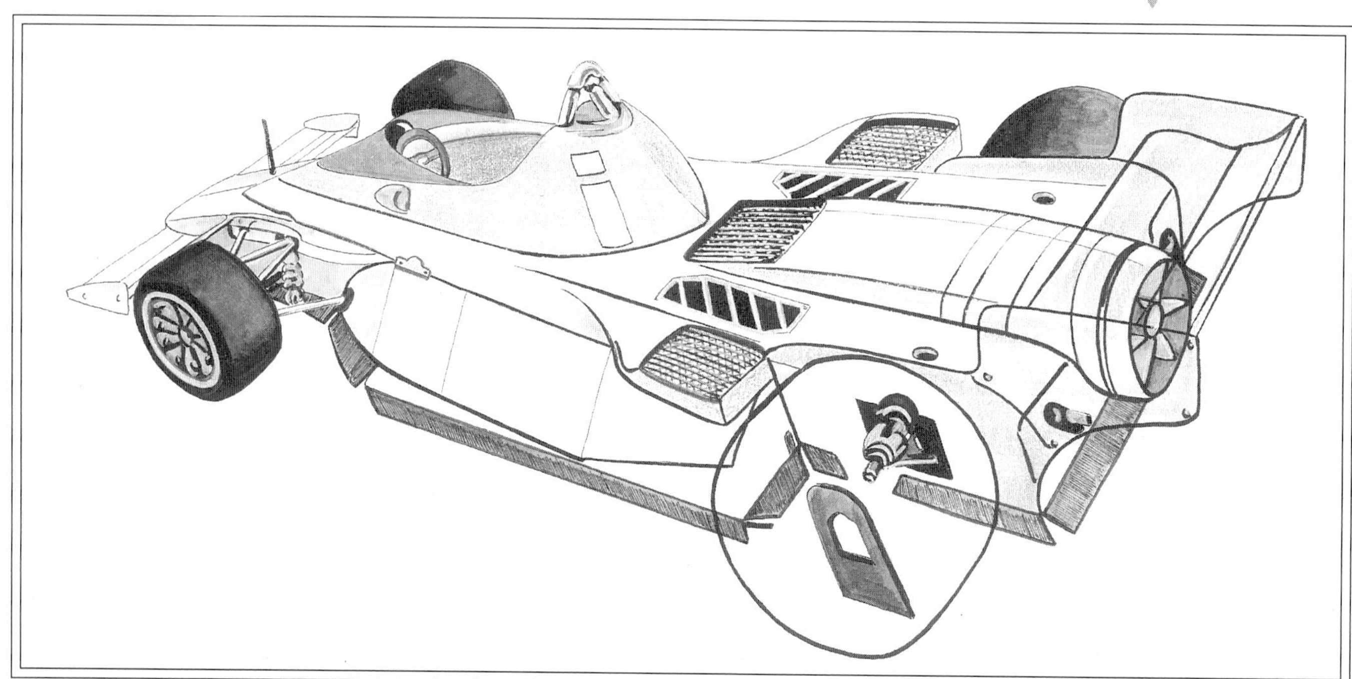

Car attempted to do mechanically what the Lotus 79 did aerodynamically. The huge fan sited in its tail, described as a cooling device, actually sucked air from beneath the car. Skirts fitted around the entire base of the BT46B provided an airtight seal to the track. With the rotation speed of the fan connected to engine speed, the system produced a powerful ground effect, the car visibly squatting closer to the road, even with stationary revving.

Niki Lauda drove the car to victory at Anderstorp where the fan threw out a large dust cloud behind it. Five teams successfully protested the system and the BT46B was henceforth banned from competition. The car itself was never declared illegal and the result of the Swedish Grand Prix stood, although the BT46B never competed again.

From January 1979, comprehensive and carefully phrased legislation on every aspect of F1 car design came into operation. The most complete set of rules so far detailed chassis and coachwork dimensions, construction methods, engine specifications, aerodynamics, suspension, and other contingencies such as six-wheelers and four wheel drive.

The governing body for Formula One became the Federation Internationale du Sport Automobile (FISA) in 1978, a division of the FIA. FISA set the overall length of the F1 car to 5 metres (196.85in). Rear overhang became further reduced to 80cm and front overhang could not exceed 120cm. Overall allowed width remained at 215cm with 150cm maximum for coachwork ahead of the front wheels. The 250-litre fuel capacity limit of 1973 was originally for cars that used more than one fuel tank and required that no single tank should hold more than 80-litres. As they considered that the centrally sited tanks of the wing cars were so well protected, FISA granted a waiver for single fuel cells of up to 250-litres sited in this position. In the event of in-race refuelling, FISA stipulated leak-proof couplings and fuel containers had to feature an air vent fitted with non-return valve.

Ground effect cars developed at a pace that outstripped the ability of FISA to govern dangerously high performance levels. From 1979 to 1983, fierce competition sparked a series of increasingly bitter disputes - over skirts, minimum weight, fuel mixtures and power output - between individual teams, the governing body and the political and commercial groups that represented their interests.

Brabham and Ferrari found themselves faced with the difficult task of adapting the unsuitable form of a Flat 12 to a wing car design. The wide and low-sitting Alfa Romeo and Ferrari units posed a real problem as the heads projected into the area needed for the 'venturi tunnels' under the car that produced the ground effect. Brabham opted to abandon the Alfa Romeo engine and build a ground effect chassis around the DFV. The BT48 ran modestly in mid-field all season, but the lessons learned in 1979 would be applied with great success a year later.

Ferrari stayed with the Boxer engine and designer, Mauro Forghieri's, solution was the unusual 312T4, which

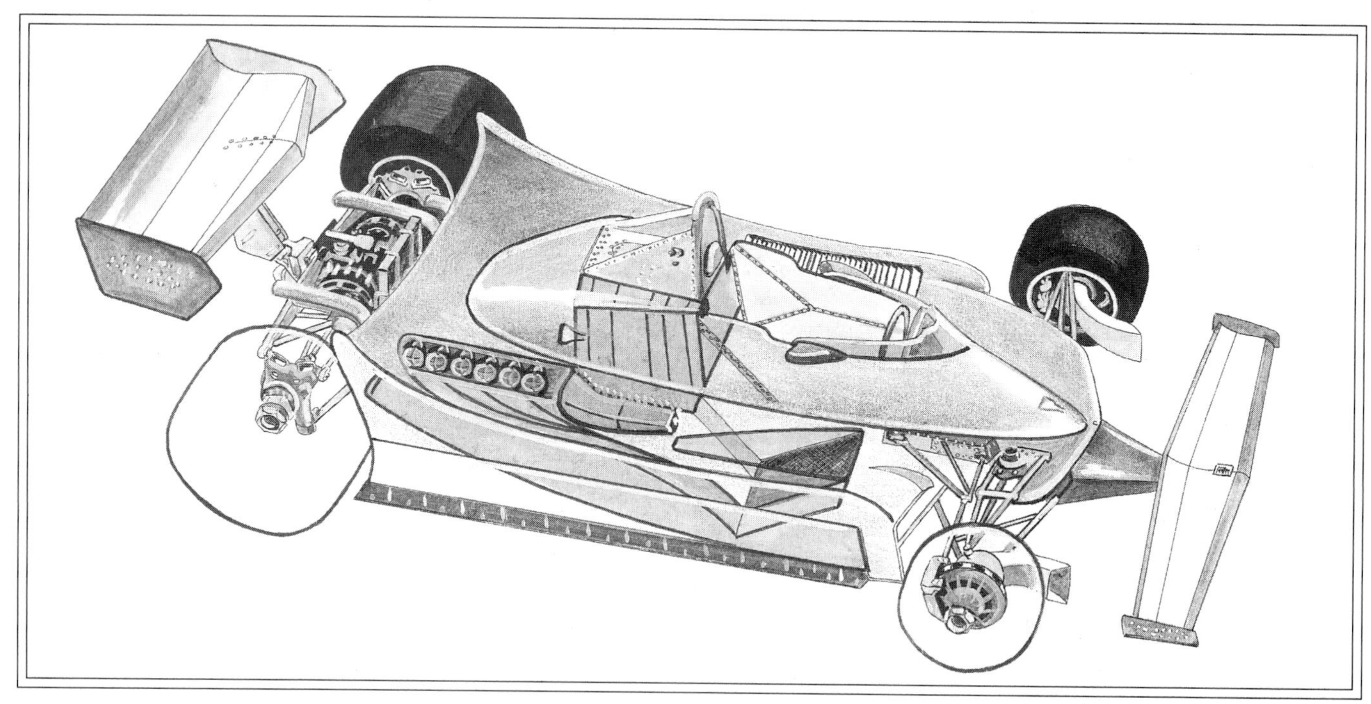

1979 Ferrari 312T4

1979 Ferrari 312T4 Street Wing

1979 Ligier JS11

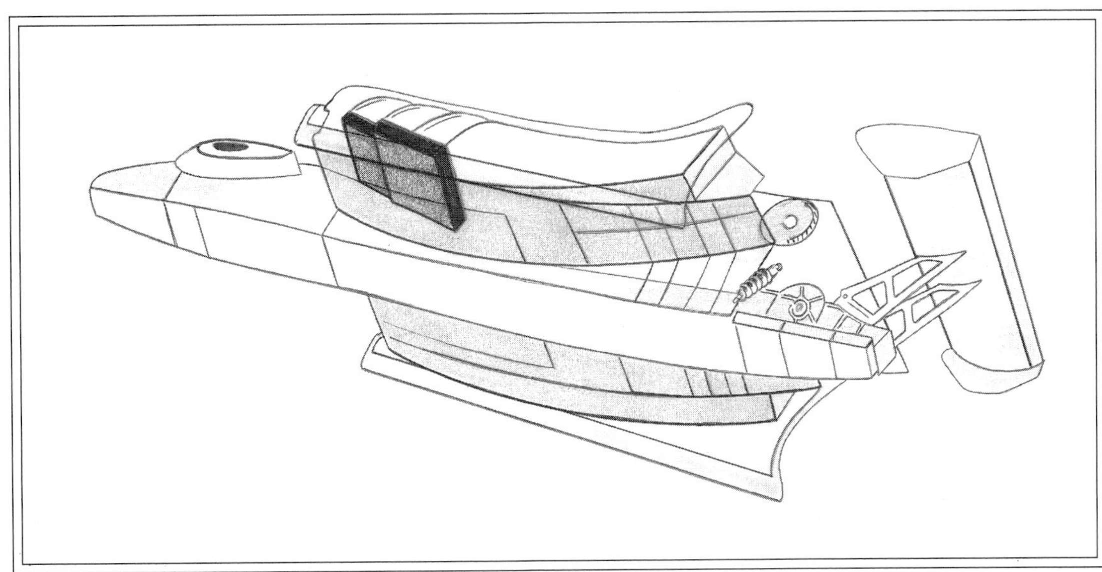

made its debut at the third race of the season in Kayalami. Conventionally, the wide sidepods carried moveable skirts, masking the undertray which curved steeply upwards towards the rear, forming the inverted wing. In addition, the 312T4 made full use of over-body surfaces to increase downforce. The design also directed airflow through the car from the wide upper body section at the front to plenum chambers sealed to the Flat 12 induction trumpets each side. Forghieri sited the oil cooler in the right hand sidepod and the water radiator in the left. A separate gearbox oil cooler was set over the engine behind the large, one-piece upper body section.

Ferrari tried a full width rear wing sited ahead of the axle line at Long Beach and Monaco street circuits. Gilles Villeneuve dominated the USA West event and team leader, Jody Scheckter, won in Monte Carlo. By working the design so hard, and also achieving an excellent level of reliability, the team was able to ensure that the 312T4 finished consistently in the points.With three wins apiece, Jody Scheckter was World Champion ahead of Gilles Villeneuve, and Ferrari took yet another Constructors' Cup.

Opinion on the aesthetic merits of the 312T4 remains divided; however, it is certain that the upgraded 312T5 was a disaster. At Montreal, the reigning World Champion even failed to qualify.

Ligier began the 1979 season with a very strong wing car design, Michel Beaujon and Gerard Ducarouge brilliantly interpreting the ground effect concept demonstrated by Lotus. The JS11 featured deeply sculptured side-pods that curved up sharply ahead of the rear wheels. Spring-loaded skirts sealed the side-pods to the track for their entire length with suspension members tucked out of the airstream. From the underside, the inverted wing profile and venturi tunnels formed either side of the slim monocoque were easily apparent.

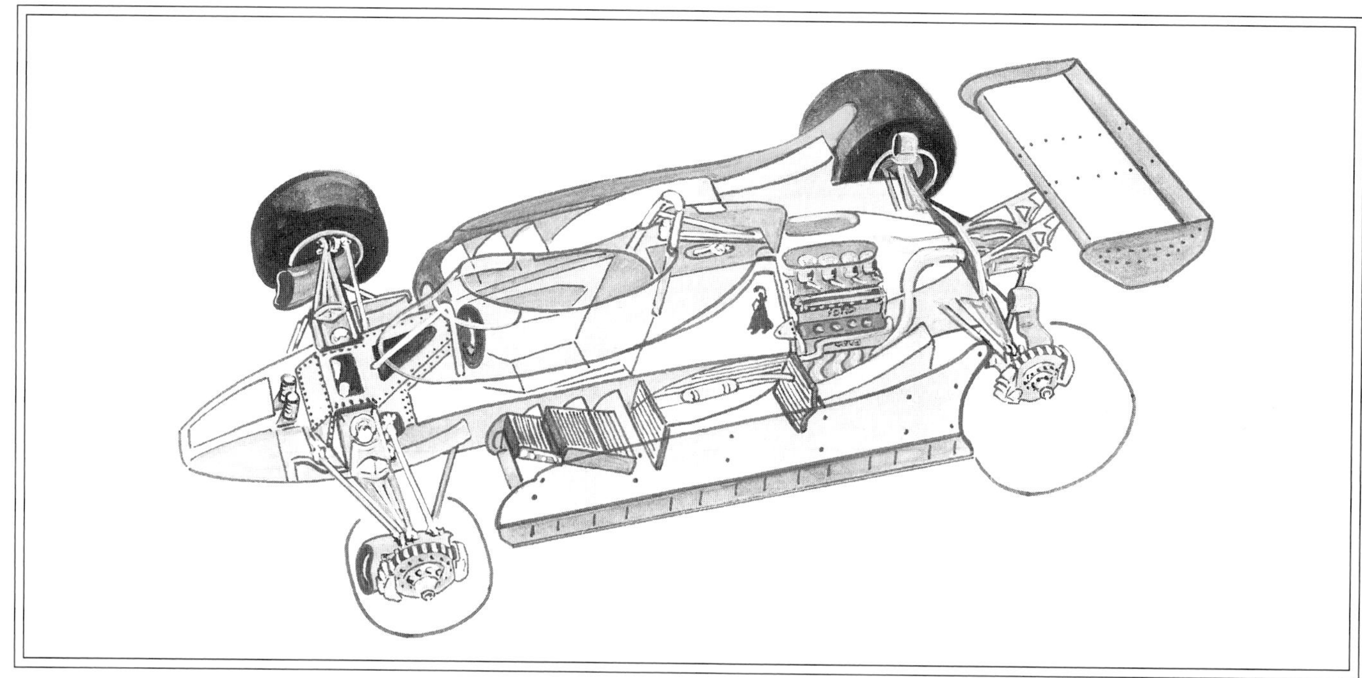

1980 Ligier JS11-15

Jacques Laffite won the opening events of 1979 in Argentina and Brazil. Three races later his Ligier team mate, Patrick Depailler, won in Spain. Thereafter, Ligier seemed to lose their way. Relocating their main testing facility halfway through the season undoubtedly cost the team vital time and progress. Running new components, such as revised side-pods, without sufficient prior testing led to inevitable failures that deprived Ligier of several potential victories.

With an upgraded suspension and new wings, the re-worked JS11-15 remained otherwise unchanged. The aluminium monocoque and central fuel cell ahead of the Cosworth DFV ensured a solid construction. Like many of the leading teams, Ligier found that levels of downforce generated by the chassis and rear wing rendered nose-

1980 Williams FW07/B

wings entirely unnecessary at the faster circuits. Ligier often demoralised the opposition with stunning qualifying performances, only to face defeat during the race. One win each for Jacques Laffite and Didier Pironi failed to do justice to such an impressive machine.

Patrick Depailler left Ligier and joined Alfa Romeo for 1980. While testing at Hockenhiem, a suspension failure threw the Alfa into a barrier at high speed, killing him instantly.

The first Grand Prix-winning car from Williams made its debut in Spain, five races into the 1979 season. Less than two months later, Clay Reggazoni, scored a memorable win at Silverstone, followed by four victories from team mate Alan Jones. The scoring system allowed only the best four results from each half of the season to count towards the championship, otherwise Jones may well have secured the title.

With the FW07, designer, Patrick Head, elegantly proved the themes established by Lotus more successfully than Lotus themselves. This light and reliable Cosworth-powered car used rocker-arm suspension above lower wishbones with inboard coil springs and dampers. New side-pods for 1980 gave the FW07B even smoother lines. Always competitive, Alan Jones and the FW07B took the World Championship with five wins. Another victory from team mate, Carlos Reutemann, assured the team of their first Constructors' Cup, with total points nearly double that of nearest rivals Ligier. A year later, during a fiercely innovative season, the FW07C challenged for the title honours right down to the last race.

By 1981 concerns over increasing cornering speeds led to an abrupt ban of the sliding skirt, the main component of the ground effect system. The rules also insisted on a clearance of 6cm

1981 Brabham BT49/C

between the lowest suspended part of a car and the track. The clearance cars of 1981 initially featured larger wings in order to compensate for lost downforce. By the third race of the season, rigid skirts, fixed to the body, began to appear.

Brabham designer, Gordon Murray, designed a way round the clearance rule, reasoning that it was unenforceable. He devised a system that he called hydropnuematic suspension. With the car moving at speed, the system bled fluid from hydraulic pistons, which replaced conventional dampers, into a central reservoir, resulting in a considerably lowered ride height. At low speed, compressed air forced the fluid back into the pistons, raising the car up on its suspension.

This suspension system allowed the Brabhams to run close to the track during a race without infringing the 6cm clearance rule when stationary in the pits. Although unreliable at first (and the subject of much protest), FISA declared the system to be legal. Because of performance advantages, other teams copied the idea until everyone used hydropnuematics. The ground effect cars had returned.

Although FISA banned sliding skirts, the rule book said nothing about fixed skirts. With a car running at reduced ride height the fixed skirts reclaimed most of the original ground effect, provided that suspension travel remained limited. Consequently, the cars became almost solidly sprung. Total wheel travel was reduced from 6.5in to just 1.5in, with tyre flexing the cause of much of that movement.

The Brabham BT49 originally appeared late in 1979. The Cosworth powered wing car used double wishbone suspension and semi-inboard springs when Nelson Piquet used it so effectively to challenge Alan Jones in the closing stages of the 1980 season. For 1981 the upgraded BT49C pioneered rising-rate suspension and a carbon panelled aluminium monocoque. Brabham also built their own transmission for the DFV. Nelson Piquet beat Carlos Reutemann to the drivers' title by one point, although the manufacturers' laurels went again to Williams because they fielded two strong drivers. Nelson Piquet was the star at Brabham and he never had a team mate capable of matching his achievements.

Because it was originally designed for six wheels, the Williams FW08 was 18cm shorter than the FW07. With rising-rate suspension and fixed skirts, Williams were able to achieve downforce levels that matched those of 1980, before the sliding skirt ban. The FW08 became the last Cosworth-powered car driven to the World Championship. Keke Rosberg achieved this with only one victory and a remarkable succession of consistent points finishes. Williams were placed fourth in the Constructors' Cup behind Ferrari, McLaren and Renault.

By close of the 1982 season, FISA realised that their legislation had failed to totally abolish the ground effect cars. With cornering speeds as high as ever, the drivers were subject to forces exceeding 9G. The limited suspension

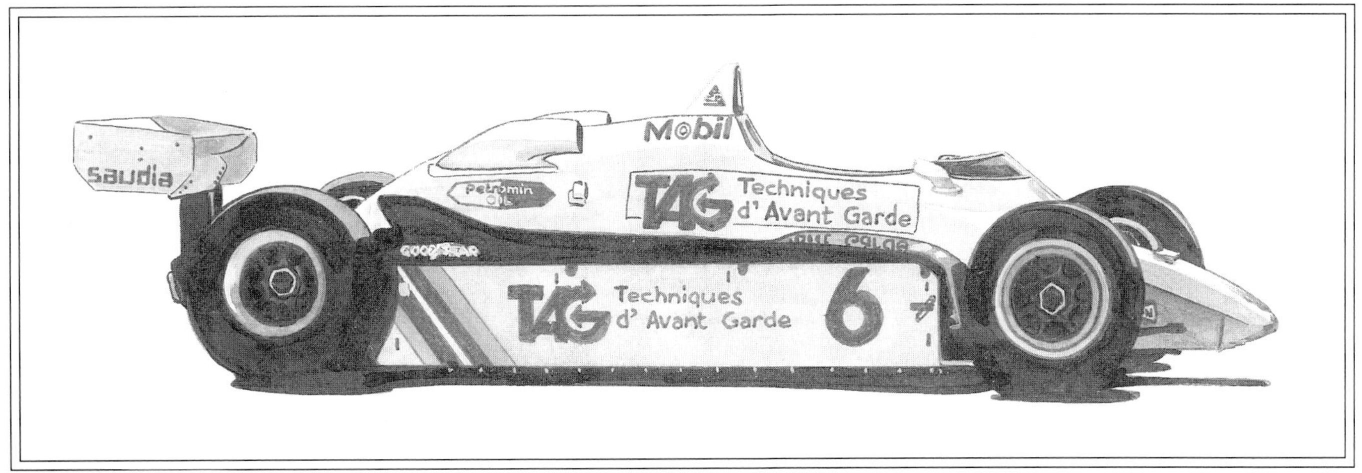

1982 Williams FW08

travel created very dangerous machines, liable to shake themselves apart, causing injuries to drivers from sustained vibration. In addition, ultra-soft qualifying tyres, which lasted for only a couple of laps, put pressure on drivers to attempt a quick lap before the tyres went off, leading - inevitably - to many accidents.

The shocking death of Gilles Villeneuve, when his Ferrari collided with a slower car during practice at Zolder, precipitated a ban on qualifying tyres and a full safety review. Tragically, Ricardo Paletti died one month later in Montreal after a start line collision in his first Grand Prix. Didier Pironi's career ended two months after that as a result of injuries sustained when his Ferrari crashed heavily during a wet practice session at Hockenhiem.

The appalling events of the 1982 season forced FISA to frame new legislation in order to conclusively outlaw the ground effect wing cars.

Chapter 16

Blind alley

Colin Chapman pioneered ground effect with the Lotus 78 and 79 F1 cars. Determined to maintain the advantage, he decided to further improve the concept. While teams like Williams, Brabham and Ligier applied the basic principles to light and uncomplicated cars with stunning success, Lotus worked to enhance downforce with increasingly complex designs. The results of this policy were disastrous …

The Lotus 80, designed as a successor to the Type 79, featured full-length skirts that extended far to the rear, making it the most smoothly faired F1 car ever seen. The intention was to derive all downforce from underside airflow and dispense entirely with external, drag-inducing wings. The completely enclosed underside even had little nose-skirts. Wind-tunnel tests

1979 Lotus 80 ▶

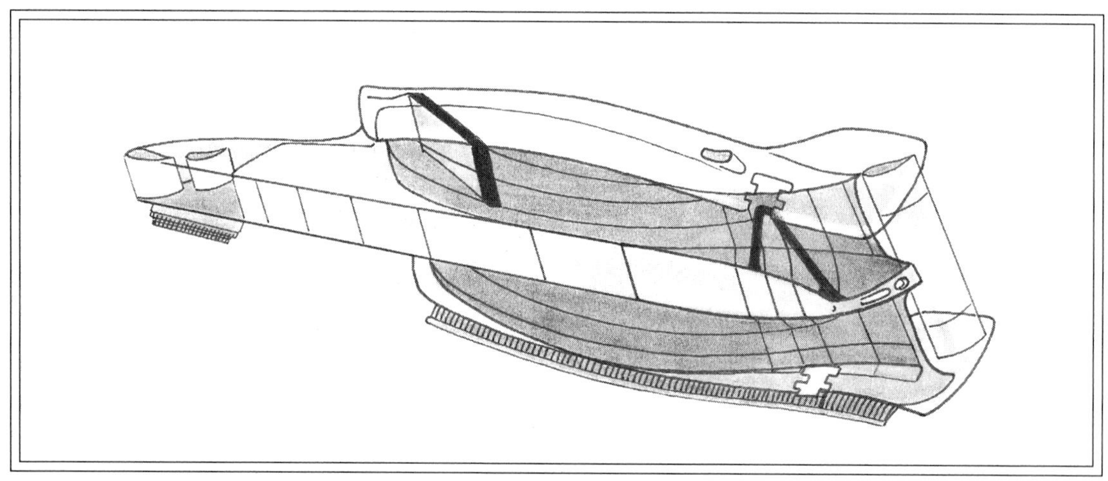

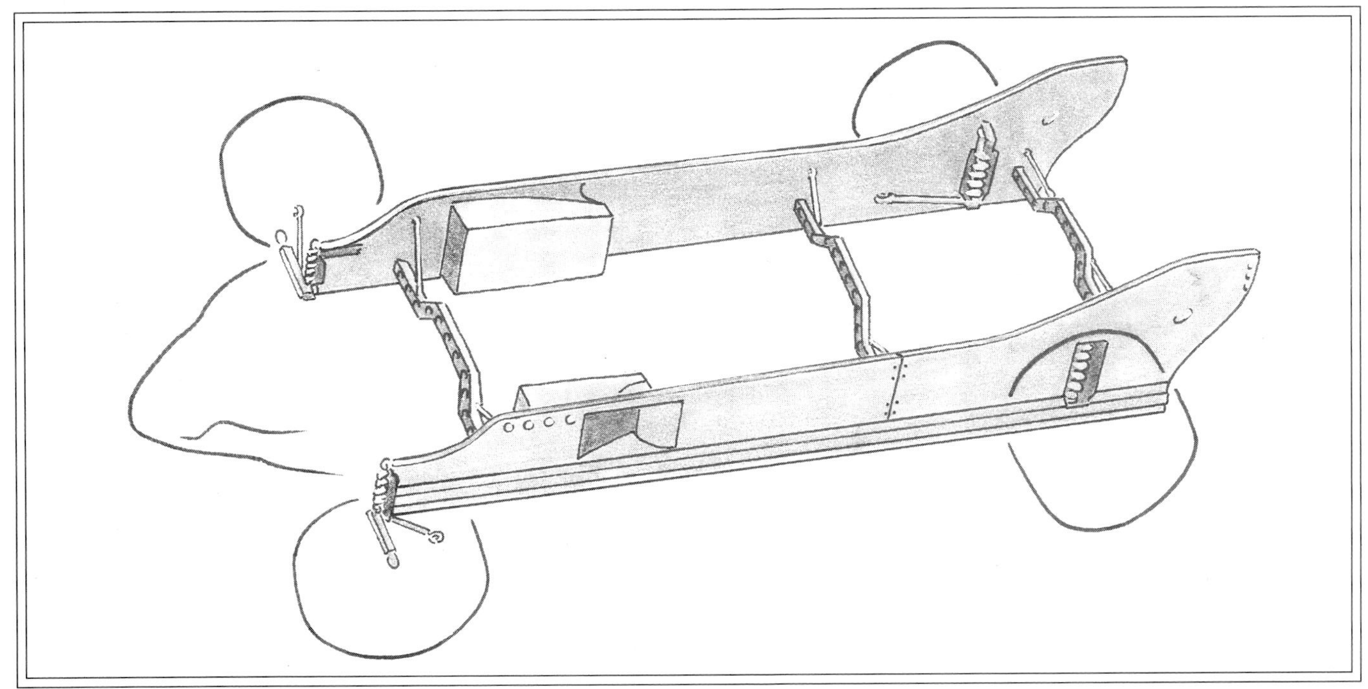

▲
1981 Lotus 88 primary chassis

suggested the possibility of a low drag, high downforce design. However, the tests failed to reveal that, in reality, the car often became unstable and difficult to control, developing a condition known as porpoising. This occurred when airflow imbalance caused a bouncing motion as the car rose and fell rapidly on its springs. All wing cars experienced porpoising to some degree,

1981 Lotus 88 secondary chassis
▶

but, usually, this was eliminated by adjusting the set-up.

The problem with the Lotus lay in the fact that ground effect over such an extensive area varied with the attitude of the car. Under acceleration, extra downforce transferred to the rear, causing understeer. Under braking, downforce transferred to the front, causing oversteer. When the car pitched in a turn, one sidepod pulled the car down more than the other, making it totally unbalanced. Lotus added wings to the nose, shortened the sidepods and eliminated the troublesome curved skirts, which enabled them to make modest progress with the design. As the ground effect era progressed, however, the fundamental flaw in the design caused Lotus to fall further behind.

Colin Chapman believed that the answer to the handling problems of the Lotus 80 lay in isolating the downforce from the other forces acting on the car. The fiendishly clever, twin-chassis Lotus 88 provided the solution. A primary chassis, containing bodywork, skirted side-pods and wings, generated the downforce. Attached to each wheel upright by coil-damper units, this assembly acted directly upon the suspension.

The independent secondary chassis comprised the kevlar monocoque, Cosworth transmission and radiators, and handled all dynamic loading through the suspension, whilst remaining isolated from the aerodynamic loads.

On its appearance at the opening race of 1981 in Long Beach, the Lotus 88 caused a record eleven protests. The principle objection was that the primary chassis constituted an illegal mobile aerodynamic device. Colin Chapman contested this assertion, gaining support from the RAC, but the protests continued until the governing body ruled that the Lotus 88 and all its derivations were illegal.

Despite having much to commend it, the rules precluded the Lotus 88 from competition. Colin Chapman had explored a blind alley, being left to watch as other teams succeeded using the concepts he pioneered.

1981 Lotus 88

Chapter 17 Forced induction

The turbocharger is an exhaust-driven impeller that pumps air under pressure into an engine. Like the (usually) belt-driven supercharger, the turbo enables an engine to burn a richer mixture than a normally aspirated unit.

The 3.0-litre formula contained a provision for turbocharged engines, restricting capacity to 1.5-litres. Undeterred, Renault entered Formula One in 1977 with a Gordini-derived V6 turbo. The team did not contest the full season and entered only one car the following year, before embarking upon a fullscale assault on F1 from 1979. The RS10 suffered from poor reliability, although the team scored an emotional maiden victory at the French Grand Prix.

The Renault RE20-25 enabled Jean-Pierre Jabouille and Rene Arnoux to collect a further three wins. It ran strongly whilst it survived but, more often, component failure led to frustrating retirements.

In 1981 the much-improved RE30 demonstrated its advantage in terms of power. Alain Prost took advantage of increased reliability with three victories. Alain and team mate, Rene Arnoux, enjoyed a competitive season that placed Renault third in the title chase.

The 90 degree V6 turbo used more space in a chassis than the normally aspirated competition. The turbos, attached to the exhausts, needed extra plumbing for the pressurised air and large heat-exchangers: a severe weight penalty compared to the lighter V8 users. Ferrari and Alfa Romeo also introduced turbocharged engines during 1981, escalating the power race.

1982 regulations called for greater driver protection in the form of a reinforced survival cell which surrounded the cockpit area. This comprised a pedal cage, deformable

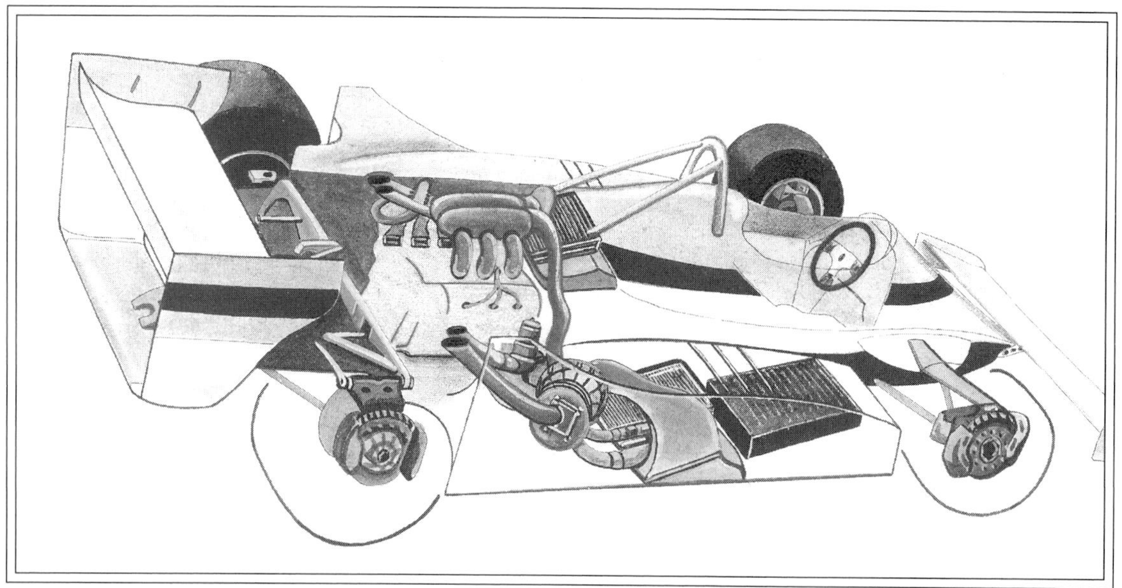

1981 Renault RE30

front structure, double thickness forward monocoque, steering fixed to upper chassis, front and rear roll-bars fixed to the chassis base and reinforced safety uprights each side of the cockpit.

The Cosworth could not compete with the power output of the turbos, so the V8 wing cars relied on better reliability and reduced weight. Indeed, British teams tried several ruses, such as fitting internal ballast tanks and dumping excess fluid during the race, which put the cars well under the minimum weight limit and caused acrimonious disputes with the turbo teams when discovered.

In-race refuelling was popularised in 1982, as the powerful turbo cars burned a lot of fuel and the weight of a full tank put them at a disadvantge in the early laps. The Cosworth teams also applied the strategy of a mid-race top-up as it was often important to ensure that the cars would be heavy enough to pass the post-race scrutineering.

The Ferrari 126C2 became the first turbocharged car to win the Constructors' Cup. Considerably revised from the previous year, the longer wheelbase housed a fore and aft gearbox, replacing the transverse unit. The 120 degree V6 used twin KKK turbos and Lucas-derived fuel injection. The suspension comprised top rocker-arms and lower wishbones. Ferrari tried many alternative locations for the ancillary mounts, radiators and intercoolers as the team tested for the optimum layout during the season.

1982 Ferrari 126/ C2

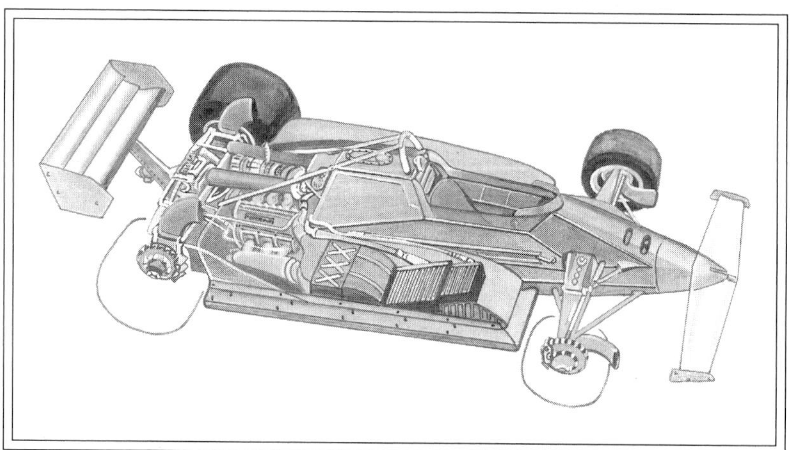

Chapter 18

Flat bottoms

The new legislation of 1983 dictated that the underside of all F1 cars form a uniformly flat plane between the front and rear wheels. This left no scope for ground effect, although engine and gearbox casings became increasingly smoothly faired. Designers sought to limit weight and improve airstream penetration by reducing frontal area; in most new cars sidepods became much smaller.

The Brabham BT52 was an extreme example of this reasoning. Since 1981, Brabham had tested and developed the

1983 Brabham BT52 ▶

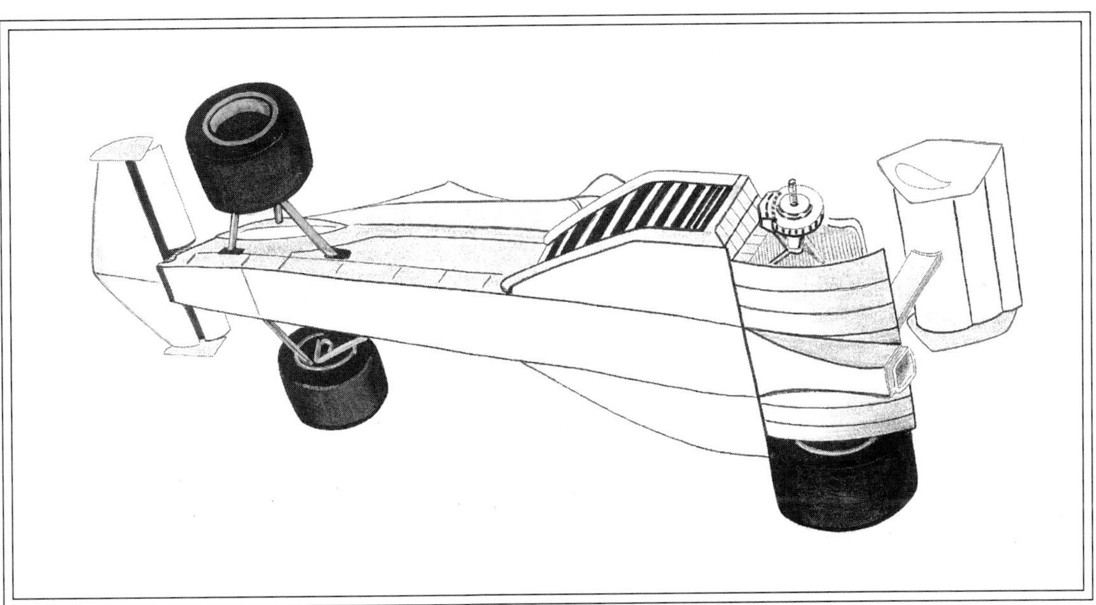

BMW four cylinder turbo, with the American designed Wiesmann gearbox, racing the BMW-engined BT50 alongside their Cosworth-powered BT49D in 1982. The slim monocoque of the BT52 housed the obligatory central fuel cell between drastically reduced sidepods. Underside bodywork extended far to the rear, where it curved sharply upwards to form a vital diffuser beneath the rear wing. Like all other teams, Brabham applied larger front and rear wings.

The Williams FW08C also featured greatly reduced sidepods. Still with Cosworth power, Keke Rosberg and Jacques Laffite struggled in the wake of vastly superior turbo cars that produced over 600bhp compared with 520bhp from the best DFVs. The nimble car felt most at home on the street circuits, Keke Rosberg securing a memorable win at Monaco and second place at Detroit. He also achieved second place in Brazil, only to be subsequently disqualified after receiving an illegal push-start outside the pit area.

Nelson Piquet secured his second World Championship with the new flat bottomed Brabham, whilst Ferrari achieved a second consecutive Constructors' Cup. Alain Prost lost the drivers' title by only two points and left Renault to begin an enduring and fruitful association with McLaren.

Race officials verified adherence to the flat bottom ruling by checking that the cars presented a fully flat surface between the wheels when viewed from beneath. When Brabham and Williams introduced small, flat fixtures each side of the monocoque base of their slender 1983 cars, many observers pondered their function. Eventually it was pointed out that the mirrors of the BT52 and FW08C projected from the straight sides of the cockpit and were visible from beneath the car, potentially infringing the letter of the law. The tiny plates were not a new aerodynamic breakthrough, they simply hid the mirrors from view!

1983 Williams FW08C

Chapter 19 Under pressure

1984 Ferrari 126/ C4

▼

In 1984 a desire to curb power levels by promoting fuel economy led to a reduction in maximum allowable fuel capacity from 250-litres to 220-litres, along with a ban on in-race refuelling. The F1 teams began using huge mobile refrigerators to cool the fuel, before filling the cars as late as

▲ **1984 Williams FW09**

possible before the race started. With boost control regulated from the cockpit, engineers and drivers worked to a strategy to maximise performance against economy. With little or no margin for error, cars often crossed the finish line only to gasp to a halt a few yards on! Leading contenders sometimes expired before completing the last lap, leading to dramatic and unpredictable results.

Ferrari further revised their design, the delta form of the 126C4, with huge rear wing and abbreviated side-pods, exemplifying the shape of the era. Winglets extended from the main rear wing to provide added downforce, the turbos having the power to compensate for the drag imposed by these massive structures. Michele Alboreto's single win at Zolder signalled that Ferrari were losing ground to other engine manufacturers. Around 900bhp was required to run competitively and the alloy-block V6, originally designed for 700bhp, often blew itself apart under the demands of increasingly high boost pressures.

Williams acquired Honda engines for 1984 and Patrick Head designed the brutal, purposeful-looking FW09 to house the Japanese V6 turbo. Keke Rosberg was the main strength of the team in this development year, winning brilliantly at Dallas on a crumbling track surface, despite the inherent throttle-lag of the Honda turbo.

Throttle-lag occurred as turbine rotation slowed, whenever the driver had to lift off the accelerator. Power dropped considerably and the turbine

1984 McLaren MP4/2

would have to wind back up to speed when the accelerator was depressed again. This led to a lag in engine response, as boost pressure built, before the engine kicked in with full power. Improved impeller design reduced the problem considerably in later turbos.

Ron Dennis gained control of McLaren in 1981, through his Project Four racing concern, and set about rebuilding the ailing team with the help of his talented designer, John Barnard. Astutely assessing current trends, McLaren, too, forged a link with an engine manufacturer.

McLaren worked closely with Porsche to design and build a 1.5-litre turbo, with Techniques d'Avant Garde funding the program. The 80 degree V6 used twin KKK chargers to produce over 750bhp during initial tests in 1983. The John Barnard designed MP4 had already raced successfully in recent years with a DFV, so Porsche built the new engine to fit an already proven chassis, the main structure of which - along with wings and brakes - largely comprised carbon composites. Other teams emulated the pinched 'Coke bottle' waist of the McLaren in succeeding years.

In 1984, Ron Dennis fielded a McLaren team of remarkable strength. The MP4/2 proved fast and reliable in the hands of two of F1's finest drivers. With turbo experience from Renault, Alain Prost displayed uncanny sympathy with his cars; driving smoothly and precisely in a style that earned him the nick-name of 'professor', he achieved seven victories in 1984. Double World Champion, Niki Lauda, a renowned technician, performed with even greater consistency. Despite only five outright wins, he secured a third title from Alain by half a point. With twelve victories

1985 Williams FW10

from sixteen races, McLaren won the Constructors' Cup by a huge margin.

New regulations in 1985 banned the rear winglet extensions, to the relief of many who regarded the 1984 Grand Prix cars as uniquely ugly. Frontal impact crash testing of chassis became mandatory, with the front section and nosebox required to withstand an impact of 750kg at a velocity of 10m/s.

In a more balanced season Lotus and Ferrari made good progress. The British team introduced turning-vanes to reduce front wheel turbulence, the feature soon becoming commonplace. Three years after the dreadful events of 1982, Manfred Winklehock was killed during the Canadian Grand Prix.

Williams challenged hard as the power delivery of the Honda turbo became smoother, further evolution of the unit enabling both Keke Rosberg and Nigel Mansell to achieve two victories. The FW10 adopted carbon composite construction throughout.

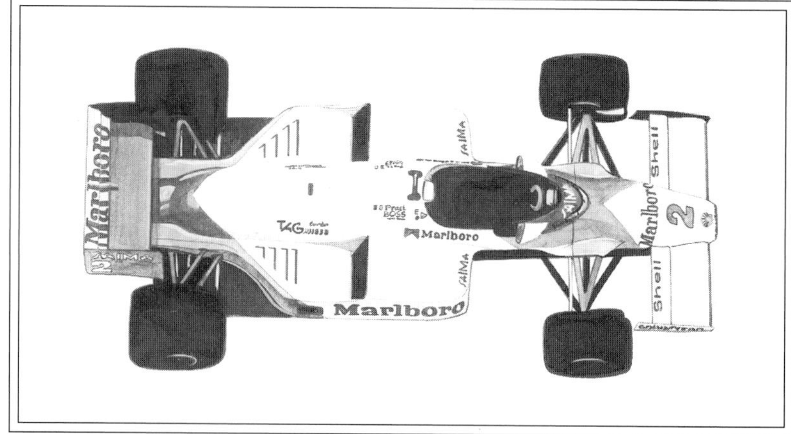

1985 McLaren MP4/2B

McLaren switched from Goodyear to Michelin tyres for 1985. New wings and minor alterations to the engine constituted the main changes to the MP4/2B. With five wins to Niki Lauda's single victory, Alain Prost gained his first title; McLaren also finished at the top of the results table.

The FIA imposed a further fuel capacity restriction, of 195-litres, for the 1986 season. Williams largely ironed out the brutal on-off power curve of the

1986 Williams FW11

Honda to produce a more driver-friendly unit. The Honda RA163, an 80 degree V6 with twin IHI chargers, also achieved vastly improved fuel efficiency. By this time, kevlar and carbon fibre universally replaced aluminium as the standard materials for construction, demonstrating greater strength and rigidity with lower overall weight.

The FW11 assumed a dominant role in the face of strong competition from McLaren, Lotus and Ferrari, taking the Constructors' Cup in 1986 and 1987. Nelson Piquet, recently joining Williams from Brabham, scored four wins in 1986. Tragically, his replacement at Brabham, popular Italian, Elio de Angelis, died when his car crashed during a testing session at Paul Ricard in France.

Nigel Mansell achieved five victories and looked certain to attain the World Championship in the final event at Adelaide when his left rear tyre exploded. Fears about the state of Nelson's tyres prompted Williams to call him in. With his fourth win in the final race, a delighted Alain Prost captured his second successive title, in the McLaren MP4/2C.

The 1987 FW11B included computer-controlled active suspension. The system, pioneered by Lotus the previous year, extended the concept of earlier rising-rate suspension with the addition of accelerometers to measure wheel movement and inertial platform motion. Onboard computerised instrumentation processed the sensor information and instructed a hydraulic reservoir to direct fluid to the appropriate hydraulic actuators. As a result, the car reacted extremely quickly

1987 Lotus 99T

▲ **1988 McLaren MP4/4**

to track surface conditions and maintained a consistent ride height and pitch, similar to the way the muscle structure of an animal reacts to balance and control its body.

More noticeable exterior changes to the FW11B included revised front wing end plates and large turbo air-intakes on each side-pod that had become quite fashionable among the leaders. Nelson Piquet won his third World Championship after a season-long duel with Nigel Mansell.

The active suspension Lotus 99T benefited from Honda engines and the awesome talent of Ayrton Senna, who won convincingly in Detroit and Monaco. He dominated the Monte Carlo event, winning six times in the seven year period from 1987 to 1993.

The FIA announced a new lateral impact test for 1988 and a ban on turbochargers to apply the following season. In the interim, normally aspirated engines of up to 3.5-litres could compete, laying down the basis of a new formula for 1989.

For the last turbocharged season Honda reworked their V6, supplying McLaren in favour of Williams, and also continuing to support Lotus. Designer, Steve Nichols, modified the McLaren, moving the radiators forward and giving the MP4/4 ram air-scoops for the IHI turbos and high front wing end plates.

Ayrton Senna joined the team and won eight Grands Prix to the seven of Alain Prost. The pair were first and second in the Championship. McLaren scored more Constructors' Cup points than all of the remaining teams put together, totally overwhelming the 1988 series with fifteen victories from sixteen events.

Chapter 20

The 3.5-litre Formula One

The normally aspirated 3.5-litre Honda V10 of 1989 produced 700bhp, a level that exceeded the first Renault turbos of the previous decade. By this time, however, 700bhp represented a power drop of over 200bhp compared to turbos of recent years. While manufacturers worked to develop the engines, designers concentrated on aerodynamics and suspension. With tyre technology continuing to advance, F1 cars were

1989 McLaren MP4/5

soon lapping the circuits faster than ever.

The MP4/5 carried the Honda V10 within smoother lines, clothed by new impact-resistant materials and aerodynamic refinements such as an advanced tail diffuser through which exhaust gases were vented into the airstream. The upswept rear diffusers of F1 cars had become essential to the downforce properties of the chassis, and teams began to pay similar attention to the design at the front. Noses became narrower, allowing larger, more elaborate wings designed for greater downforce and clean airflow over the front wheels.

Ayrton Senna won six Grands Prix to Alain Prost's four in 1989, but the French driver took the title before leaving McLaren for Ferrari. McLaren added another Constructors' Cup to their trophy cabinet before repeating

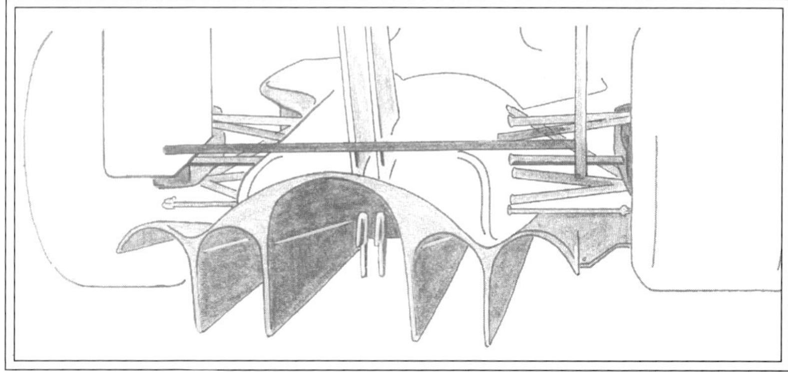

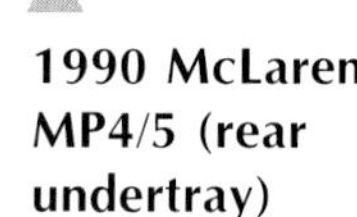

1990 McLaren MP4/5 (rear undertray)

the exercise the following year, this time Ayrton's six wins securing his second title.

By this time the rules obliged the teams to carry onboard TV cameras, the tiny sophisticated boxes sited in various locations about the chassis. In addition, further impact tests of the complete chassis and fuel tank were demanded, stimulating the development of increasingly complex mixtures of Kevlar and Nomex honeycomb to ensure

1990 Ferrari 641

continued on page 97

1951 Alfa Romeo 159 (Juan Manuel Fangio). The 1.5-litre supercharged Alfetta, with its grinning radiator and large drum brakes, dominated the first postwar Formula One World Championships.

1952 Ferrari 500 (Alberto Ascari). The 2.0-litre Ferrari proved virtually unbeatable after introduction of the restrictions that effectively ended supercharged competition.

1958 Cooper T43 (Stirling Moss). The first mid-engine car of modern Formula One led to a revolution in F1 car design.

1993 McLaren MP4/8 (Ayrton Senna). McLaren introduced aero-fences and sought to improve front end downforce with the steep curve of the nose underside.

1996 Williams FW18 (Damon Hill). Sporting a fully raised nose, wide cockpit padding, aero-fences and winglet fairings to define the optimum form of the late nineties.

1997 Ferrari 310B (Michael Schumacher). Ferrari have returned to form, their latest design demonstrating increasingly complex aerodynamics.

structural strength. Cockpit areas were made wider and 10cm higher. FISA set race duration at 305km, or two hours, whichever was reached first, and also imposed a limit on the number of practice laps allowed during qualifying.

The 1990 Ferrari 641 V12 used an electro-hydraulic gearchange operated from paddles on the steering wheel, a system which is now universal in F1. The pairing of Nigel Mansell with Alain Prost was Ferrari's most successful for several years: with six wins between them, Ferrari finished second to McLaren in the Constructors' Cup.

A major rule change in 1991 placed more emphasis on the value of a Grand Prix victory as points were now awarded as follows; 10-6-4-3-2-1.

Honda produced a new 3.5-litre, 60 degree V12 for McLaren in 1991, which they mounted in a chassis with revised monocoque, suspension and aerodynamics. McLaren also adopted semi-automatic transmission. After seven victories, Ayrton Senna easily topped the points table for his third title, even handing the lead of the final event in Japan to team mate, Gerhard Berger, whilst McLaren attained a fourth successive Constructors' Cup.

The Williams Renault V10s achieved five successive Constructors' Cup victories from 1992 to 1996, beginning with the Renault RS3 V10 in the FW14B chassis. Nigel Mansell returned to Williams in 1991, challenging Ayrton Senna strongly with five victories in the Williams-Renault FW14. The legendary Senna-Mansell duels continued the following year, with Nigel winning through to attain the World Championship after a record nine victories.

The Renault RS3 67 degree V10 produced 770bhp at 14,500rpm. Like its contemporaries, the FW14B featured an airbox for ram-air induction at high speeds. The widespread use of carbon composites now applied to the

1991 McLaren MP4/6 ▶

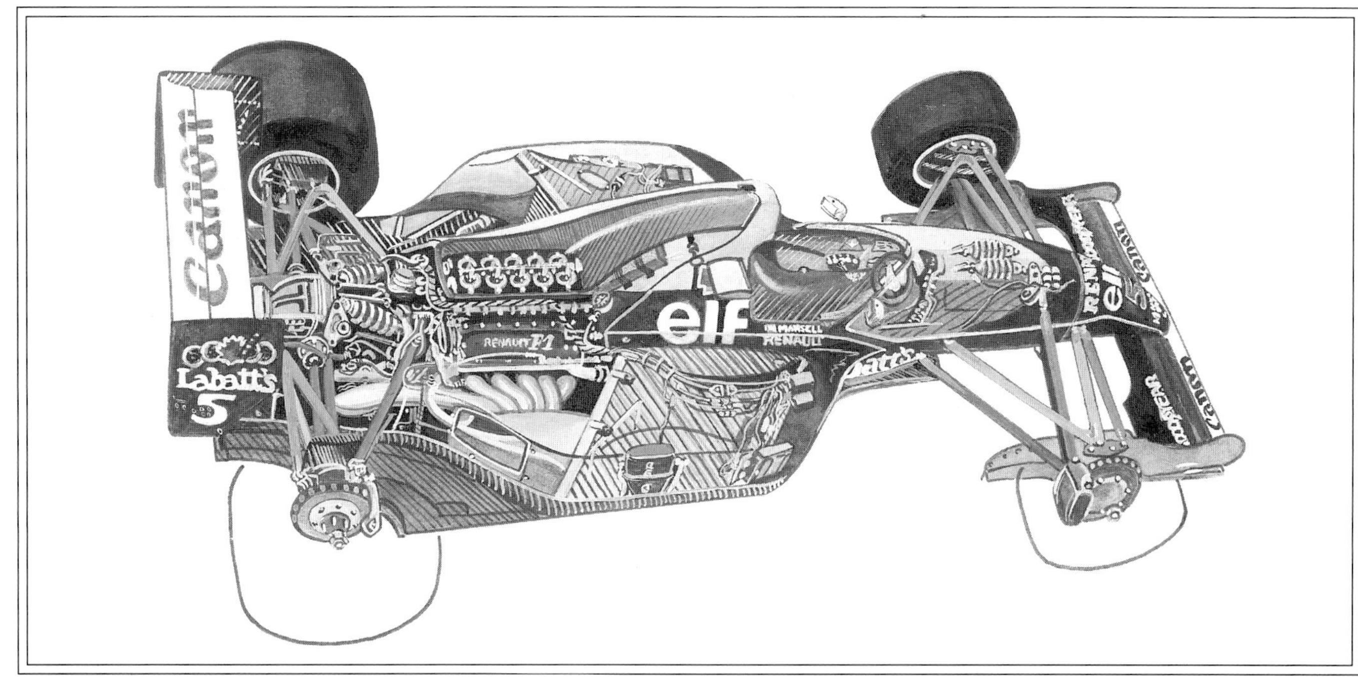

suspension, the light and extremely strong materials enabling more slender constructions combined with gas dampers tightly fitted at the top of the nose section and far inboard over the rear suspension. The carbon fibre brakes were effective at far higher temperatures than conventional alloy discs. In line with current trends, the front wings faired upwards ahead of large brake cooling scoops and turning vanes.

Alain Prost returned in 1993 after a year in retirement to take his fourth title with the Williams FW15C. In a class of its own, the FW15C was the most

▲ **1992 Williams FW14/B**

1993 Williams FW15/C

1994 Williams FW16

sophisticated F1 car ever raced. Pneumatic valve actuation and light-weight pistons gave the Renault RS5 V10 around 800bhp, and the engine management system synchronised revolutions to gearchanges, eliminating wheel-spin. The driver operated the six-speed sequential gearbox, as either a manual or semi-automatic, from finger-tip paddles on the steering wheel, while throttle control was 'fly by wire' with no mechanical linkages. The active suspension settings could also be adjusted from the cockpit.

For 1994, the FIA allowed in-race refuelling, enforcing strict equipment regulations, and banned most of the computerised driver aids, including active suspension and anti-wheel-spin devices.

Williams looked very strong at the start of the year with Ayrton Senna driving the new FW16. His subsequent death in May at Imola, following the

1994 Benetton B194

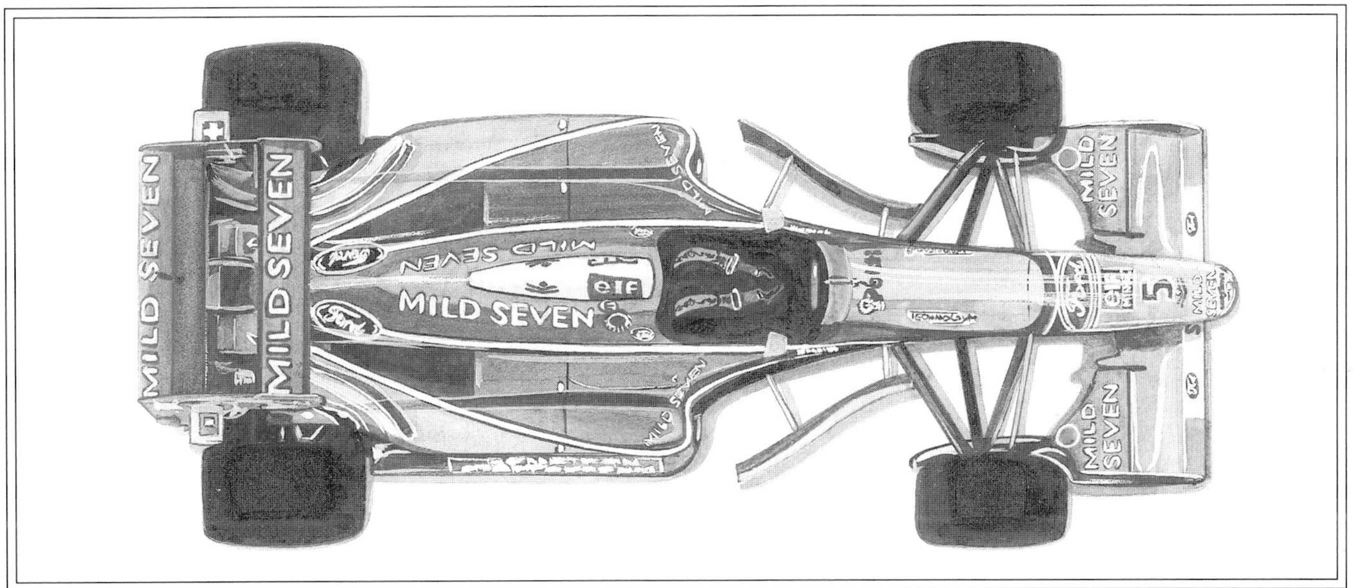

fatal accident of Roland Ratzenberger the previous day, robbed the sport of its greatest exponent and deeply shocked not only the team but the whole world. In the unreal atmosphere that followed, Ayrton's team mate, Damon Hill, and Benetton star driver, Michael Schumacher, pulled Formula One together with a championship chase that continued all season until a controversial collision finally resolved the title in the German's favour.

Regarded as a lively, twitchy car, the B194 uniquely suited Michael Schumacher's aggressive driving style. The high-revving 3.5-litre Ford Zetec-RV8 supplied sufficient pace to take on the Williams. The most striking aspect of the car was its raised, shark-like nose section and barge boards, or aero-fences, that resulted from the frantic search for aerodynamic advantage in the wake of the turbo ban. Rear wings were also becoming more complex, featuring anhedral forms arranged in many complex layers.

The 1994 season was the last of the 3.5-litre era. With massive power outputs and improved aerodynamics, the F1 car had become faster than ever.

For 1995, the governing body decided to revert to a 3.0-litre normally aspirated formula, with no provision for turbochargers.

Chapter 21

Raised noses and aero fences

Tyrrell - and later Jordan - pioneered raised noses with anhedral wings in 1991. A raised nose, coupled with an effective rear diffuser to suck air away from the tail, encouraged faster airflow under the car, thereby lowering air pressure and increasing downforce. Over successive years, the design led to the trend of raising the nose still higher and suspending the front wing beneath it. Benetton applied the highest nose to the B193 in 1993; within four years it became a universal feature of F1

1991 Jordan 191 (nose wings) ▶

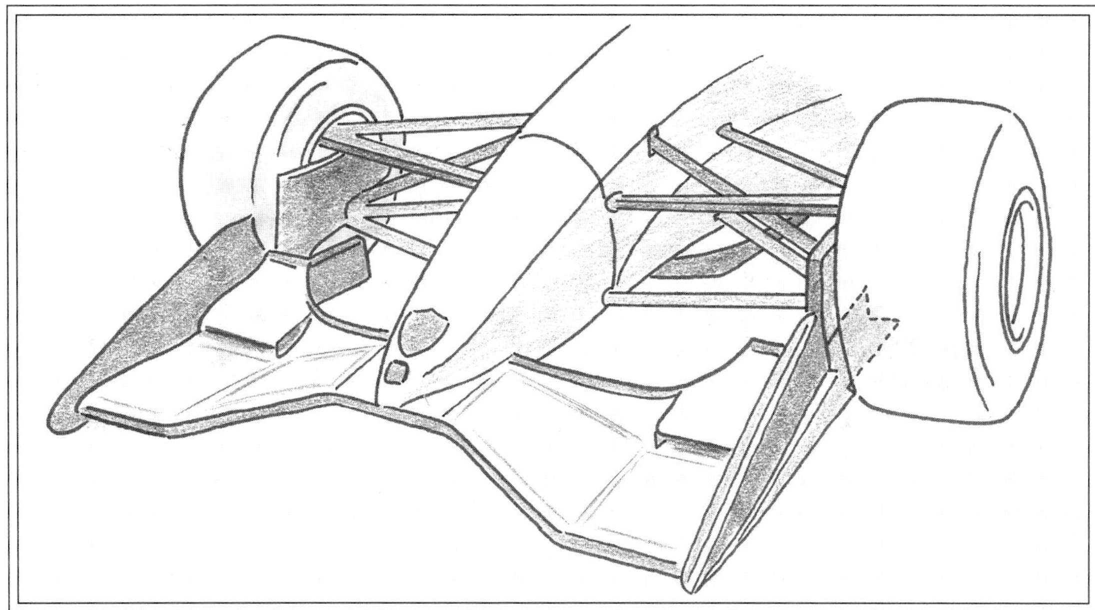

design.

In the same year McLaren introduced outrigged fences to direct airflow off the front tyres away from the rear wing. The aero-fence, which considerably smoothed overbody airflow, enabling the aerodynamic surfaces to work more effectively, was soon adopted by all F1 teams.

McLaren, along with the majority of teams, adopted a nose section that curved sharply upwards underneath the car, beyond the extent of the front wheels and into the area required by FISA to form a uniformly flat plane. In order to keep the cars legal, designers extended the flat base of the car to cover the curve and present a flat underside right up to the front wheels. The projection, called the shadow-plate, quickly also became a standard feature of modern F1 cars.

After Honda's withdrawal from Formula One, McLaren used the Ford HB 75 degree V8 fitted with TAG engine management. Despite all the latest computerised systems, the car was never in the class of the Williams, which made Ayrton Senna's wet weather victories at Interlagos and Donington all the more remarkable. He

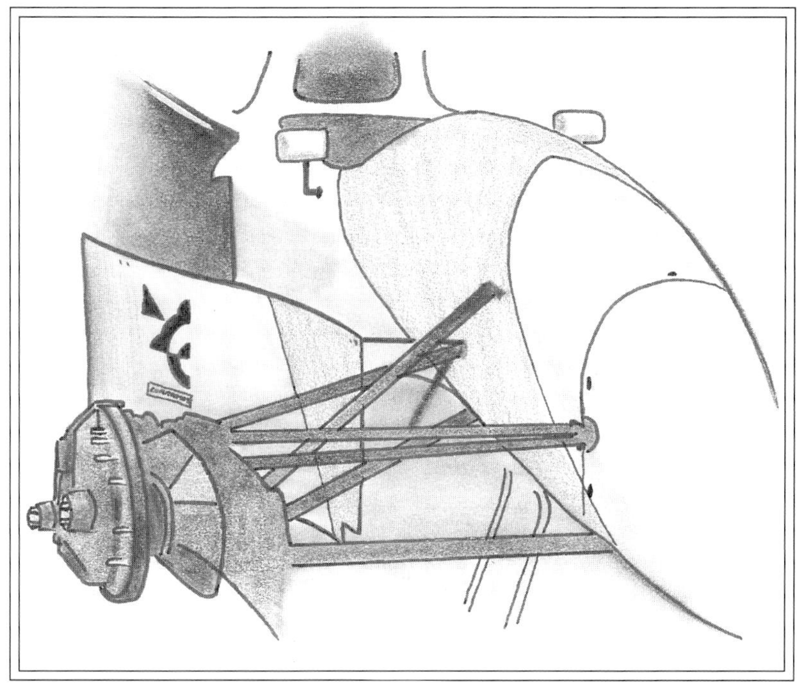

▲ **1993 McLaren MP4/8 (aero-fence)**

1993 McLaren M4/8 (shadow-plate) ◄

1993 Benetton B193 (aero-fence) ▶

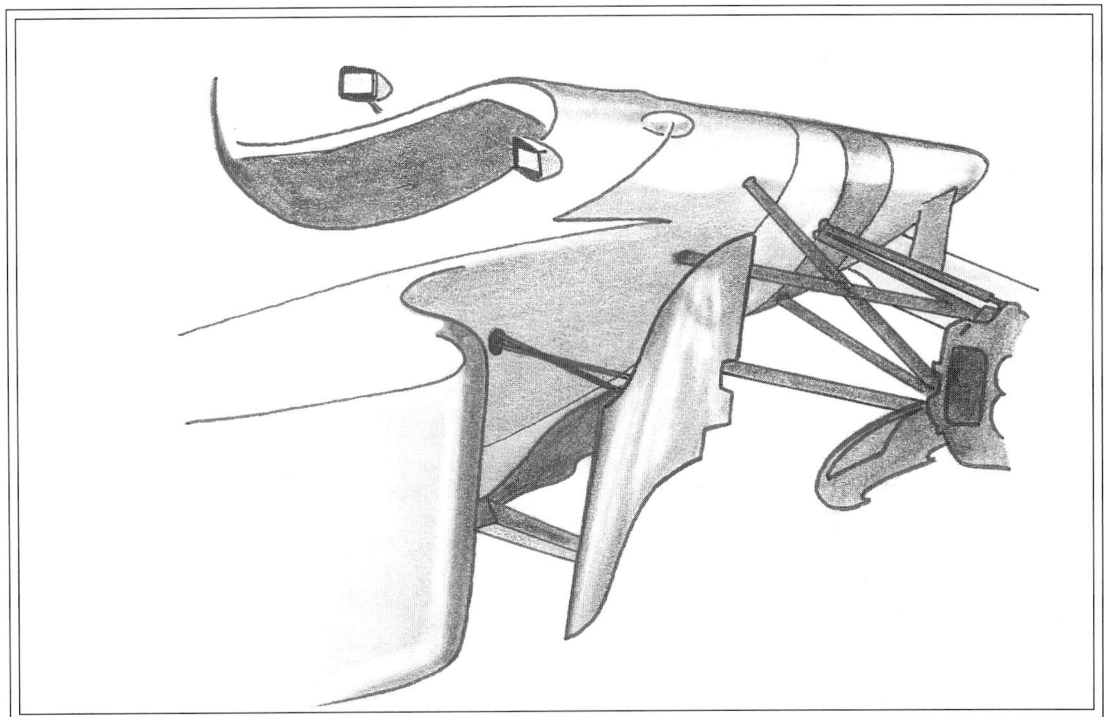

also won in Monaco, Japan and Australia, to achieve second place to Alain Prost in the championship.

Most teams eventually emulated the Benetton form with its high raised nose, suspended front wings and outrigged aero-fences. However, many designers, whose giant egos were matched only by those of the drivers, claim they arrived at the optimum design completely independently ...

Chapter 22 The 3.0-litre V10

For the 3.0-litre formula of 1995, Benetton secured the use of Renault engines. Even with reduced capacity, the Renault V10 remained the finest Formula One engine and Benetton felt able to engage Williams on equal terms.

The B195 used an anhedral rear wing similar to Williams's and several different front wing arrangements, with either curved or straight leading edges. Rear winglets were back in fashion, although not the illegal extensions from the top of the wing end plate banned ten years previously. The new winglets extended from the lower part of the end plate to fixtures on each sidepod, just ahead of the rear wheels. In addition to

1995 Benetton B195

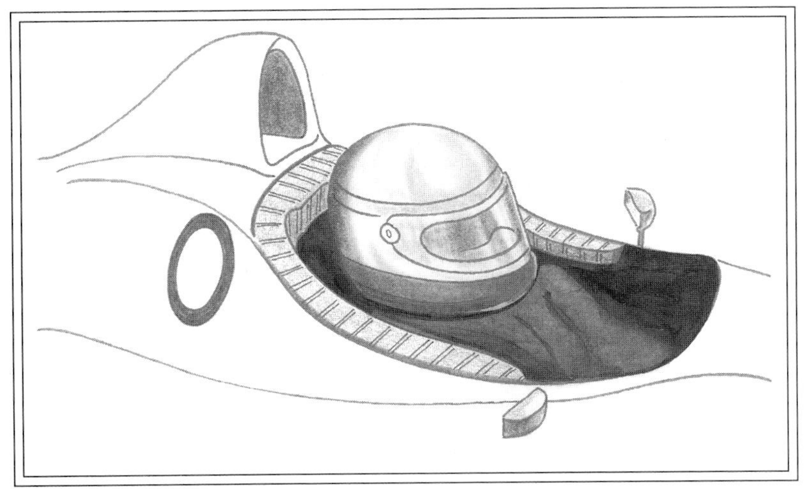

▲ **1996 Cockpit protection**

benefiting downforce, they acted as fairings for the rear wheels, guiding airflow smoothly over them and greatly reducing turbulence.

The Hill-Schumacher battle resumed in 1995 and the closely fought contest continued all season. Finally, with the title decided in his favour, double World Champion Michael Schumacher left Benetton for Ferrari and a new challenge.

An FIA safety advisory group, under the direction of chief medical delegate, Professor Sid Watkins, concluded that additional cockpit protection should be mandatory for the 1996 season. Similar to the high-sided Indycar cockpits, the new designs featured extensive padding that was criticised for limiting driver peripheral vision and adversely affecting airflow. More recent designs have incorporated this requirement quite smoothly, however, and drivers have adjusted to reduced lateral visibility.

Ferrari's powerful V10 and lightweight carbon composite chassis returned them to front running status in 1996. Michael Schumacher added fresh impetus to the development program - and team morale - as he drove the car to victories and points finishes, despite being beset by appalling reliability problems. His mastery of the car during a wet Spanish Grand Prix was particularly impressive.

1996 Ferrari 310 ▼

1996 Williams FW18

During the previous year Williams had fully raised the nose of their FW17, almost to a horizontal position, along with everyone else except Ferrari, who adopted the form mid-way through 1996, and McLaren, who have maintained a lower nose profile. The Renault V10 remained the most potent power plant in Grand Prix racing, putting the 1996 FW18 in a class of its own as the similarly-engined Benetton team had somewhat lost its way.

Most interest in Formula One centred on which of the Williams drivers would win the World Championship. Both men were famous sons; Jacques Villeneuve joined Damon Hill after winning the Indycar series in the USA and closely contesting the championship during his first season in F1. At the final event in Japan, Damon won the race and the title in decisive fashion, already knowing he had lost the Williams drive for 1997.

Chapter 23 Towards 2000

Most of the 1997 generation F1 cars use 3.0-litre V10s from eight different engine manufacturers: Renault, Ferrari, Mercedes-Benz, Peugeot, Ford, Mugen-Honda, Yamaha and Hart. Engine performance in terms of power and efficiency, with consequent affects upon aerodynamic set-up, tyre choice and strategy, remains a deciding factor in maintaining the competitive edge.

Computer-aided design and wind tunnel testing are now standard requirements. Carbon fibre composites comprise all of the chassis components and F1 structures are stronger and more rigid than ever before.

The latest aerodynamic forms have presented new complications regarding chassis design: the Benetton B197 failed to generate enough heat in the tyres to make them effective, whilst the new Ferrari tends to oversteer on entry to a corner and understeer halfway

1997 Ferrari 310B

1997 Williams FW19

through. This imbalance, most notable on circuits with high speed corners, may be the cause of both 310Bs suffering wheel-bearing failure during the British Grand Prix at Silverstone.

Williams remain top of the field with the new FW19, the latest evolution Renault V10 capable of out-distancing the other units for straight line speed and reliability. With great determination, Michael Schumacher matches their pace, despite the handling difficulties of the 310B; his peerless ability may soon bring Ferrari their first World Champion driver since 1979.

Multiple World Champions Jackie Stewart and Alain Prost have entered F1 as team operators, their experience paying off handsomely in terms of guiding the new teams towards fine performances. McLaren have returned to form with David Coulthard winning the Australian and Italian Grands Prix in the Mercedes-Benz powered MP4/12.

The most recent developments

1997 McLaren MP4/12

range from electronic balancing of braking effect to each wheel, through actuators similar to those in previous active suspension systems, to small additional nose-vanes, the benefit of which is not immediately obvious.

FISA may soon ban rear winglets, although most teams have now adapted their side-pod configuration to produce a raised fairing that is not actually a winglet.

Smaller, treaded tyres are to be introduced shortly, accompanied by a reduction in chassis width. The smaller tyres are the subject of much debate; that they are designed to improve safety and enhance racing quality there can be no doubt. However, many argue that, with *less* grip, the cars will hardly be safer ... Proponents of tyre size reduction point out that, lower break-away speed in corners will lessen the energy of an impact, and drivers are likely to adjust to longer breaking distances once they have tested the performance envelope of their car. Treaded rubber would, of necessity, comprise a harder compound that is less prone to contamination from dust and debris off the racing line, which will increase scope for overtaking. The way in which the post-race scrutineers will enforce the rules on tread depth is not yet fully understood, but perhaps some kind of scanner will be devised.

Electronic components will probably continue to shrink - cameras might become unnoticeable. Further improvements in materials technology could offer opportunities to save weight or chassis space, creating more room for aerodynamic restructuring. Experimental carbon fibre engines have already been built and alternative fuels may also be developed.

Despite recent advances it is not likely that F1 cars will ever be running on sunlight, but they may become more

Futurecar

smoothly faired as designs continue to evolve.

The author's concept of Futurecar as illustrated features smaller, treaded tyres and a narrower chassis. The side-pods curve upwards at the rear, compensating for the lack of winglet fairings. The front wing hangs beneath a slimline raised nose, ahead of the aero-fences.

As we have seen, chassis design alone will not determine how effective the new car is. The greater variety of engines makes choice critical, and the right driver, too, remains crucial to the package.

What will constitute the next major breakthrough and again alter the shape of the Grand Prix car? Gradual enhancements are expected, but a fantastic evolutionary leap forward is not foreseen; then again, were any of the advances over the years predictable?

Index